SADLIER
FAITH AND
WITNESS

LITURGY AND WORSHIP

A Course on Prayer and Sacraments

Rev. Thomas Richstatter, O.F.M., S.T.D.

William H. Sadlier, Inc.
9 Pine Street
New York, New York 10005-1002
http://www.sadlier.com

Acknowledgments

Scripture selections are taken from the *New American Bible* copyright ©1991, 1986, 1970 by the Confraternity of Christian Doctrine, Washington, D.C. and are used by license of the copyright owner. All rights reserved. No part of the *New American Bible* may be used or reproduced in any form without permission in writing from the copyright owner.

Excerpts from the English Translation of the *Catechism of the Catholic Church* for use in the United States of America, copyright ©1994, United States Catholic Conference, Inc.—Libreria Editrice Vaticana.

Excerpts from the English translation of *The Roman Missal* ©1973, International Committee on English in the Liturgy, Inc. (ICEL); excerpts from the English translation of *Rite of Penance* ©1974, ICEL; excerpts from the English translation of *Rite of Confirmation*, Second Edition ©1975, ICEL; excerpts from the English translation of *Ordination of Deacons, Priests, and Bishops* ©1975, ICEL; excerpts from the English translation of *Dedication of a Church and an Altar* ©1978, ICEL; excerpts from the English translation of *A Book of Prayers* ©1982, ICEL; excerpts from the English translation of *Documents on the Liturgy, 1963-1979: Conciliar, Papal, and Curial Texts* ©1982; excerpts from the English translation of *Order of Christian Funerals* ©1985, ICEL. All rights reserved.

The English translation of the Gloria in Excelsis, the Sursum Corda, the Sanctus, the Lord's Prayer, and the Gloria Patri by the International Consultation on English Texts (ICET). All rights reserved.

Excerpt from TURN! TURN! TURN! (To Everything There Is a Season), words from the Book of Ecclesiastes, adaptation and music by Peter Seeger, TRO ©Copyright 1962 (renewed) Melody Trails, Inc., New York, N.Y. Used by permission.

Quotation reprinted from JULIAN OF NORWICH: SHOWINGS, translated by Edmund Colledge, O.S.A. and James Walsh, S.J. ©1978 by The Missionary Society of St. Paul the Apostle in the State of New York.

Cover Illustrator: Glynnis Osher
Text Illustrator: Genine Smith: 9, 25, 41, 56, 65

Photo Credits

Jim Saylor
Photo Editor

Lori Berkowitz
Associate Photo Editor

Diane J. Ali: 115 right.

Art Resource: 27 left, 74; Scala: 38 right; Erich Lessing: 80.

Lori Berkowitz: 42 bottom foreground.

Boltin Picture Library: 34, 36, 110–111, 116 center and left.

Bridge Building Images/ Robert Lentz: 115 left, 116 left.

Karen Callaway: 99.

Myrleen Cate: 50 top, 68 top, 84 top, 96 left.

Carr Clifton: 62–63.

Catholic News Service: 114 left.

Comstock: 49, 106–107.

Crosiers/ Gene Plaisted, OSC: 18, 26 all, 32, 33, 35 background, 42 top left, 50 left, 52 both, 54 right, 55 both, 58 bottom, 66 right, 72, 76 top right, 84 bottom, 91 top, 92 both, 108 right, 114 center, 119 both.

FPG: D. Dietrich: 38 left; Miguel Sanchez: 103; Bill Losh: 106 center.

The Franciscans: 31 bottom.

Ken Glaser: 58 top.

Granger Collection: 42 bottom background, 89, 120–121 bottom border.

Anne Hammersky: 16, 30 right, 35 foreground, 43 left & center, 50 right, 75, 88, 96 right.

Image Bank/ Harold Sund: 12; Siquis Sanchez: 54–55; Anthony Boccaccio: 56; Stephen Marks: 108 left; Michael Melford: 112.

Institute for Our African Ancestors: 114 right.

International Stock/ Tom Stamm: 76 background.

Ken Karp: 30 left, 40.

Gamma Liasion/ Livio Anticoli: 94–95.

Ron Mamot: 54 left.

Maryknoll: 115 center.

Masterfile/ Courtney Milne: 8–9.

Minden Pictures/ Frans Lanting: 6–7.

National Geographic/ Raymond Gehman: 86–87.

Our Lady of the Most Holy Rosary Catholic Community, Albuquerque, NM: 51.

Sarma Ozols: 64.

Panoramic Images/ Koji Yamashita: 122–123.

Photo Edit/ Michael Newman: 42 top right, 43 right.

Photo Researchers/ Worldsat: 70–71 background.

Photonica/ Myra Kramer: 79; Yasushi Kurada: 102–103.

Picture Perfect/ Warwick Buddle: 78–79.

H. Armstrong Roberts: 63.

St. Joseph's Abbey/ Br. Emmanuel Morinelli, OCSO: 83.

James Schaffer: 82, 90.

Nancy Sheehan: 17, 31 top.

Chris Sheridan: 66 left, 68 right, 76 bottom left, 91 bottom.

Jacquline Srouji: 57.

Stock Market/ Joseph Sohn: 46–47.

Superstock: 19, 24, 106 left.

Sygma/ G. Giansanti: 70–71 foreground.

Tony Stone Images/ Gary Holscher: 10 left, 23 bottom left, 31 background; Hugh Sitton: 10 bottom; George Grigoriou: 10 top; Paul Chesley: 10–11; M. Townsend: 22 top left, 23 center right; Ralph Wetmore: 22 top right; David Olson: 22 center right, 23 bottom right; John Noble: 22 center right; William J. Herbert: 22 bottom right; Liz Hymans: 22 bottom left, 23 top right; Kevin Morris: 23 top right; Robert Daemmerich: 76 left; Zigy Kaluzny: 118; Emmanuelle Dal Secco: 120.

Uniphoto: 14–15.

Garth Vaughn: 120–121 top border, 122 left.

Viesti Associates/ Bavaria: 104.

Westlight/ W.Warren: 48–49.

Bill Wittman: 27 right, 40–41, 59, 65, 68 left, 81.

General Consultant
Rev. Joseph A. Komonchak, Ph.D.

Official Theological Consultant
Most Rev. Edward K. Braxton, Ph.D., S.T.D.
Auxiliary Bishop of St. Louis

Publisher
Gerard F. Baumbach, Ed.D.

Editor in Chief
Moya Gullage

Pastoral Consultant
Rev. Msgr. John F. Barry

Scriptural Consultant
Rev. Donald Senior, C.P., Ph.D., S.T.D.

General Editors
Norman F. Josaitis, S.T.D.
Rev. Michael J. Lanning, O.F.M.

Catechetical and Liturgical Consultants
Eleanor Ann Brownell, D.Min.
Joseph F. Sweeney
Helen Hemmer, I.H.M.
Mary Frances Hession
Maureen Sullivan, O.P., Ph.D.
Don Boyd

"The Ad Hoc Committee to Oversee the Use of the Catechism,
National Conference of Catholic Bishops,
has found this catechetical text to be in conformity
with the *Catechism of the Catholic Church.*"

Nihil Obstat
✠ Most Reverend George O. Wirz
Censor Librorum

Imprimatur
✠ Most Reverend William H. Bullock
Bishop of Madison
November 3, 1997

The *Nihil Obstat* and *Imprimatur* are official
declarations that a book or pamphlet is free of
doctrinal or moral error. No implication is contained
therein that those who have granted the *Nihil Obstat*
and *Imprimatur* agree with the contents, opinions, or
statements expressed.

Printed in the United States of America.

S® is a registered trademark of William H. Sadlier, Inc.

Home Office:
9 Pine Street
New York, NY 10005–1002

ISBN: 0–8215-5655-X
123456789/987

CHAPTER 1

More Than Meets the Eye

At present we see indistinctly,
as in a mirror,
but then face to face.

1 Corinthians 13:12

A rock, a flower, a fire, a stream,
A touch, a smile, a good-bye, a dream—
Oh, how these are so much more than they seem!
In what ways can things such as these be
"much more than they seem"?

The Real World

You are about to enter into a whole new way of looking at life and faith. Now that you are more mature, it is time to go deeper in understanding exactly what Christ meant when he said, "Where two or three are gathered together in my name, there am I in the midst of them" (Matthew 18:20).

Jesus is with us, especially when we gather to celebrate the liturgy. But how does this happen? To begin our challenging exploration, we must get back to basics and start with our human experience of signs and symbols.

Have you ever heard the expression, "There's more here than meets the eye"? It means that often things can suggest images, emotions, or meanings beyond what we can see with our eyes. When this happens, the things become symbols. A *symbol* is something that stands for or suggests something else. *Symbol* comes from a Greek word that means "to throw together." When something we observe with our senses is "thrown together" with the unseen—a memory, a feeling, or an idea—it can become a symbol.

How does this happen? To answer this question let's take a look at fire. The discovery of fire was an earthshaking moment in human history. And down through the centuries the image of fire has become a symbol of great power. Human beings see in fire so much more than simple scientific combustion. Fire has many symbolic meanings: light, energy, safety, warmth, even godlikeness.

Over time and cultures certain things or acts have come to have deeper meanings that are recognized by the people of that culture. There is a kind of "sign language" that uncovers a

Sacred Space

We can see from the signs that have been left us that ancient peoples used symbols to express their deep beliefs and concerns about the great mysteries of life, concerns that we share today: Who are we? Who made us? Why are we here? Who directs our lives? Does anyone care for us?

This awareness of the divine, the holy, the sacred appears in every human culture. It is expressed differently in different cultures; but in all of them, symbols are part of the way we humans communicate our belief in the sacred. And just as we do today, the ancient peoples set aside symbolic *places* in which to celebrate the sacred mysteries of life.

In every age and culture, the holy place—a shrine, forest grove, temple, church—has been symbolically set apart as a sacred area.

The ancient Greeks saw their highest mountain, Mount Olympus, as the dwelling place of the gods, where they lived shrouded from men's eyes by the mists. The Athenians chose the highest hill in their city, the Acropolis, as their sacred place.

The remains of Machu Picchu, the sacred city of the Inca, lie at the top of the Andes mountains, close to the heavens and suggesting symbolically the efforts humans must make to approach the sacred.

Have you ever been to a place sacred to a culture other than your own? If so, share your experience.

deeper world of meanings, ideas, and emotions. That sign language is made up of symbols. A multicolored piece of cloth, as we have seen, arouses feelings of patriotism. A dove suggests the human desire for peace.

Among all the creatures of earth, we humans are the only ones who have the power and the imagination to think symbolically, to interpret and make sense of our lives, and to express in symbols our deepest beliefs and concerns. What does all that have to do with our Catholic faith and with this course on liturgy and worship?

You're about to find out. This book will invite you to celebrate your faith in a way you have never done before. It will challenge you to look at things you thought were familiar in a whole new way.

What about us? What do our sacred places symbolize? Our sacred places and spaces express our deepest beliefs as Catholics. Our most profound belief is that Jesus Christ, the Son of God, became one of us. He suffered, died, and rose again so that we might have new life. All our sacred places, objects, and actions help us to enter more deeply into this mystery of our salvation through Jesus Christ.

Symbols in Action

It is 1963. An assassinated president is being laid to rest. President Kennedy's flag-draped coffin is brought from the cathedral and placed on a horse-drawn gun carriage for the procession to Arlington National Cemetery. Behind the gun carriage a soldier leads a riderless horse. There is no music for this procession, only the sound of muffled drums and the creaking of the carriage wheels.

At the cemetery members of the military fold the flag, with solemn precision, into an intricate and prescribed triangle and present it to the widow. Three buglers play in echoing sequence the plaintive *Taps*, the sound that ends a soldier's day. Mrs. Kennedy then lights an "eternal flame," a light that will never go out, on the president's grave.

This event, indelibly imprinted on the memories of those who witnessed it, is rich in symbols. How many can you discover?

When symbols are connected like this in meaningful action, we have what is called a ritual. *Rituals*, then, are symbolic actions that often express our deepest beliefs or concerns. Some rituals, of course, are very simple, such as placing candles on a birthday cake, or giving a teammate a high five after a victory.

Other rituals, such as the funeral described above, the opening ceremonies of the Olympic Games, or a graduation ceremony, have deeper and more complicated symbolism.

For us Catholics, all our churches are sacred spaces. Each is the "house of God" because Christ is present there in the Eucharist. Your own parish church is a sacred space. Some places, however, hold deeper significance for us because of their location or because of something that happened there. St. Peter's Basilica in Vatican City is one such sacred space. From the earliest centuries of the Church, Christians believed that this was the place where Saint Peter was martyred and buried. Excavations beneath St. Peter's have uncovered a *necropolis*, a "city of the dead." Inscriptions and bones found there seem to confirm that this is indeed the burial place of Saint Peter.

What Makes a Ritual?

Anthropologists tell us that rituals, or symbolic actions, are at the heart of human experience. From earliest times human beings have developed rituals to celebrate, remember, and express in a public way their deepest concerns, their most profound beliefs. Rituals often mark transitions from one stage of life to another. They help us make sense of life's mysteries.

What are some characteristics of ritual? Here are three of the most important ones.

- Ritual is *interpersonal*. It is something one does not alone but with others who share the same beliefs or concerns. When symbolic action is expressed by people as a community, its deepest meanings are revealed and experienced.

- Ritual is *repetitive*. Humans repeat rituals because these actions express what is most constant, most meaningful in their lives. We celebrate ritually what is unchanging to us in a changing world. If an action is true and meaningful to us, it must be repeated, celebrated, over and over again.

- Ritual is *acted out*. It uses symbolic movements and gestures to express deeper meaning.

For example, do you know why the ritual of greeting someone by shaking hands arose? What to us is now an automatic action of greeting was once a very serious and very symbolic action. In the early Middle Ages, it was a sign to strangers or possible foes that one was not holding a weapon and therefore was not a threat to the other. Once men shook hands, both were committed by honor to obey its meaning and not to attack one another during their meeting. The symbol persisted into later ages, when a man's handshake was equivalent to his word. "Let's shake on it" came into the language of business and diplomacy as a symbol of one's word of honor.

 Can you describe some other symbols that are universally recognized?

An understanding of symbol and ritual is essential to a mature understanding of our worship as Catholics. All the sacraments of the Church involve ritual. And if we are aware and willing to participate, each ritual draws us more deeply into the life of faith it expresses.

In this chapter we have explored symbols: objects, places, and actions that have meanings beyond what we can perceive with our physical senses alone. All people of a given culture recognize and identify with these meanings. Of course a person has to have had some cultural experiences and a certain maturity to be aware of symbolic meanings. You are certainly ready to begin to think symbolically.

See if you can recognize the meanings of these symbols. If you are not sure, use your imagination. See how close you can come to the universal understanding of each one.

Ritual Celebrations

Like symbols, rituals, such as a salute or a handshake, can be very simple. They can also be much more complex, much richer, especially those dealing with people's cultural memories and deepest beliefs.

We have spent a great deal of time on symbol and ritual in this opening chapter. Why? Because symbolic thinking is one of the most essential and profound things humans can do. Symbolic thinking is certainly the most essential and profound thing we do as Catholics. And when we grow in appreciating and understanding the symbols and rituals of our faith, they will speak to us as nothing else in the world does.

 Describe a ritual that is part of your Thanksgiving, Christmas, or Fourth of July celebration.

Symbol	Meaning
A bishop carries a shepherd's staff. It is called a *crosier*. Why a shepherd's staff?	
A traditional symbol of justice is a statue of a woman. She wears a blindfold and holds balanced scales in her hands. What do these symbols say about justice?	

Explain this statement: Symbols can affect our memories and our emotions.

Why is an understanding of religious symbols and rituals essential to a mature understanding of Catholic worship?

Singing is a vital and vocal way to participate in the prayer of the Church. As a group talk about ways you might encourage yourselves and other young people to join in praising God in song. Perhaps the parish choir director would be willing to help you. This might also be one important way you can prepare for a Mass together later in this course.

YOU ARE MY WITNESSES

Scripture *My Life*

One beautiful way to look at symbols in Scripture is found in the story of the prodigal son (Luke 15:11–32). In this parable the father is a symbol of God. Remember when the son came home? His father *ran* to meet him. He *hugged* and *kissed* his son even before saying a word. What clearer symbols could the son have had of his father's love?

Catholic Teachings

About Sacramental Signs

The Church's sacramental celebrations involve not only signs and symbols relating to creation and human life but also to God's mighty deeds for his people, above all the Passover. Through the power of the Holy Spirit, these signs and symbols become "bearers of the saving and sanctifying action of Christ" (*Catechism*, 1189).

CHAPTER

The Prayer
of the Church

Lord, teach us to pray.

Luke 11:1

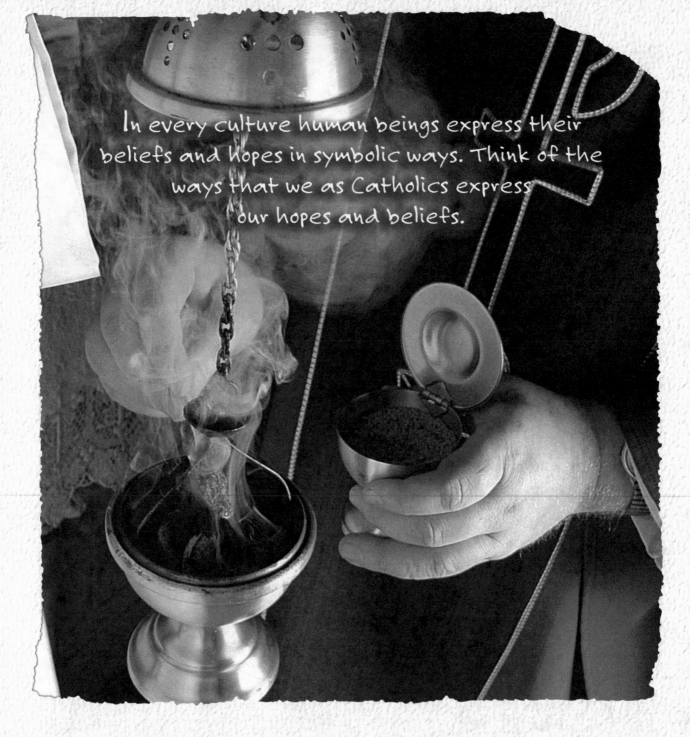

In every culture human beings express their beliefs and hopes in symbolic ways. Think of the ways that we as Catholics express our hopes and beliefs.

Catholic Symbols and Rituals

Words alone can never fully express the deep meanings of our Catholic faith. Because we are human beings, because we have bodies and live in the world of created things, we often use symbols to express our thoughts and feelings, our understandings and insights. When we Catholics pray together, we celebrate in and through *symbolic* activity. Catholic worship is filled with symbols: eating and drinking, being plunged into water and anointed with oil,

standing and sitting, processing from place to place, raising our hands, speaking out and singing together. As Catholics we must never forget that these signs and symbols of our faith put us in touch with the divine. Through them we share in God's own divine life.

The church, the sacred place where we meet for worship, is full of symbols: light, fire, water, word, incense. Often the very architecture of a church is symbolic. Many of our churches are cross-shaped in design, a symbol of our redemption. Others are circular, symbolic of the public nature of our worship.

The prayer of the Church is not only *symbolic* activity; it is also *ritual* activity. We do things over and over in prescribed, formal, and set ways. Rituals are characteristic of Catholic worship. At Mass, for example, Catholics know "what happens next," what to expect. When the priest greets us with, "The Lord be with you," we respond, without any thought or hesitation, "And also with you." When the priest invites us, "Let us pray," we stand up. Our rituals help us to do together what we came to do: celebrate Christ's saving actions in our lives.

Catholics perform many ritual actions during our liturgical celebrations. Perhaps you have never thought about the meaning of these rituals. But understanding what is being said and done through ritual helps us to participate in the prayer of the Church.

In order to pray well and to come to know what that prayer means in daily life, it is important for us to acquire the skills and understanding that are necessary to celebrate the prayer of the Church with enthusiasm and joy.

In this course we will discover how Catholics have traditionally prayed and worshiped God. We will explore the liturgy and the sacraments, the Church year, and Catholic devotions. We will learn about the rituals and ceremonies that Catholics have used through the centuries to celebrate God's presence in our lives. In this way we, too, can come to know how much we are loved by God and come to appreciate even more what it means to belong to his Church.

The Prayer of the Church

Liturgy is the public prayer of the Church in which we proclaim and celebrate the mystery of Christ. Originally the word *liturgy* meant "a public work"—literally, a work for the people, for everyone.

Because the public prayer of the Church is for everyone, it came to be called *liturgy*, which now

means "the participation of the people in the work of God." What is the work of God? It is the work of our redemption; it is what Christ did for us. Liturgy is a work by and for the people, but above all it is God's work. In liturgy the mission of Christ—the work of his passion, death, resurrection, and ascension—continues today.

Liturgical prayer, as God's work and the work of the people, the Church, is a very particular kind of prayer. What are some of its characteristics?

Public   First, as we have already seen, liturgical prayer is *public* prayer. Yet it is public in a very special way. Not all prayers said in public are liturgical. For example, a group of people may gather in church to say the rosary. This is certainly a public act, but liturgical prayer is public in a deeper sense.

Liturgical prayer is public because each liturgical celebration, such as the Mass or the sacraments, includes, concerns, and affects the whole Church community. And because liturgical prayer is always for the entire Church, it is public even when only a small number of people are present.

Prayer of Christ   Liturgical prayer is the prayer of Christ himself. Because it is the prayer of Christ, liturgical prayer has unique and special value above and beyond anything else we, as Church, could possibly do.

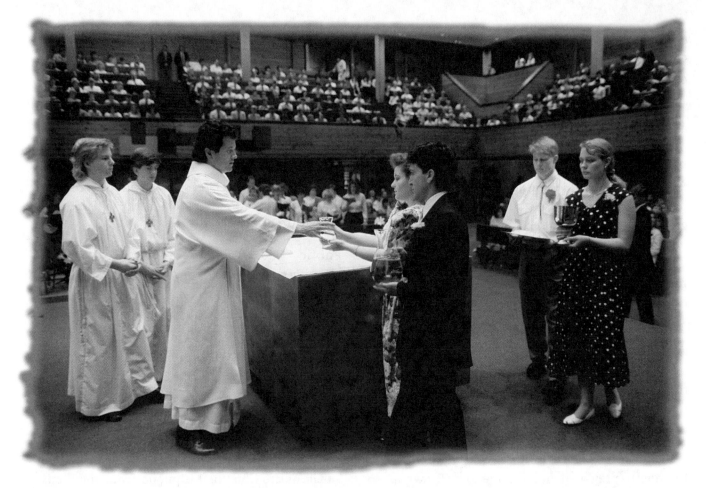

A deacon accepting the offerings of bread and wine at the preparation of the gifts

Worship of the Trinity   Every liturgical celebration is offered in, with, and through *Jesus Christ*, in the unity of the *Holy Spirit*, to the honor and glory of the *Father*. Liturgical prayer is always worship of the Trinity.

Addressed to God   Liturgical prayer is always addressed to God. Even when we honor Mary and the other saints in the liturgy, we praise and thank God for them.

In the Words of the Church   In our private prayer we are encouraged to pray freely and spontaneously, both alone and sometimes with others. In liturgical prayer, however, we pray in the words and with the actions given to us by the Church.

Communal and Personal

In the liturgy we pray with Christ, the head of the Church, and with his whole body, the Church on earth and in heaven. Now that's public!

Do you think it is possible to be both *public* and *personal* at the same time? Have you ever been with a group of people celebrating a victory, a memorial, or another special moment in life? You are all experiencing something together, but at the same time you are feeling it personally, individually.

That is what liturgy is like. It is a communal experience and a personal experience at the same time. Good liturgy is never private, but good liturgy is always personal.

Liturgical prayer is the prayer of Christ. What do you think might be some of the concerns of Christ that are expressed in the liturgy?

There is an ancient saying in the Church: "The way we pray shows what we believe." The liturgy is the official way we pray as Catholics. In what way does the prayer of the Church show what we believe?

What makes us who we are as Catholics is our relationship to the Father in and through Jesus Christ. We believe in Jesus Christ—in who he is and in what God has accomplished in him. What makes us Catholic is our belief in the paschal mystery of Jesus. By the *paschal mystery* we mean all that God has done to redeem us in Christ Jesus, especially in his suffering, death, resurrection, and ascension. We proclaim this paschal mystery at every Eucharist when we say, for example:

Christ has died, Christ is risen, Christ will
   come again.

The word *paschal* refers to Passover, the feast of freedom for the people of Israel. During this great feast, the Jewish people celebrate their deliverance, their passing over, from slavery to freedom. During Holy Week and Easter, we Christians celebrate the "passing over" of Jesus from death to new life. As the liturgy tells us, Jesus Christ is now and always "our Passover and our lasting peace."

Mystery means more than just something that cannot be fully understood. It also means *a truth that continually calls us to deeper understanding*, a truth so wonderful that we are continually drawn to investigate the depths of its meaning.

Catholics believe that the birth, life, suffering, death, resurrection, and ascension of Jesus Christ is the very center of all that exists. When Jesus passed from death to life, all of creation was made new—including ourselves. His new life is now our new life. It is the central vocation of every Christian to discover and live the meaning of the paschal mystery, Christ's passion, death, and resurrection, in today's world. How do we do this?

The first step is to begin to develop a personal relationship with God, for it is our *person* that we bring to the public prayer of the Church. We do not come to the celebration of Christ's paschal mystery as strangers in God's presence or even as mere acquaintances. We come as Jesus' own friends and disciples, just as his first followers did.

Usually friendship does not just happen. We have to work at a relationship. We have to spend time with the other person. We have to develop

common interests. We have to want what is good for the other, and we need to be willing to sacrifice for the other.

We become friends with God in much the same way, spending time with him, developing common interests, learning about God, sharing our concerns, our dreams, our hopes. That is what praying really is.

And even though we may not realize it, God is waiting for us to come to him. God, after all, tops the list of those who love us. He sees, knows, and loves us as we really are. God shows his love for us through Jesus Christ and through the Church. And it is in praying with the Church "through Jesus Christ, our Lord" that we come to recognize and respond to him in a personal way.

 What is your relationship with God like? Do you come to celebrate liturgy as a stranger, as an acquaintance, or as a friend?

The Crucifixion, Georges Rouault, 1939

A Little History

How did liturgy come to be the way it is today? Our liturgical family has a history, a rich and interesting one formed by many languages, cultures, and historical events.

What are the roots of our liturgical life? Where do these symbols and rituals come from? We begin with Jesus himself. As we shall see, it is really Jesus who gives us the sacraments and entrusts them to the Church.

When the Son of God became one of us, he did so in a particular culture: Jesus was a Jew who lived in first-century Palestine. His first followers were also Jews. After the resurrection and ascension of Jesus, they continued to pray in the Temple in Jerusalem on the Sabbath. But now they did something new as well.

We read that "every day they devoted themselves to meeting together in the temple area and to breaking bread in their homes" (Acts 2:46). In the Temple they listened to readings from the Old Testament and responded with psalms and prayers. In their homes they shared the Eucharist, as Jesus had instructed them. Even at this early date, we can trace the origin of the two parts of the Mass as we know them today: the Liturgy of the Word and the Liturgy of the Eucharist.

As the good news of Jesus spread from Palestine to the ends of the Roman Empire, the message was translated into new languages and planted in new cultures. Greek was the common language spoken at that time, so the gospels and the letters of Saint Paul were written in Greek. Later, when Latin became the official language of the Roman Empire, the Bible and the liturgy were translated into Latin.

In what ways do we still celebrate the liturgy as the early Christians did? How are we different?

We no longer go to the Temple for prayer; instead we go to our parish churches. But we still read the same readings and pray the same psalms as the first Christians did. We no longer read the Scriptures in Latin, as the Romans did; now we read them in our own languages. We celebrate the same breaking of the bread, the same Eucharist. The most important parts of the liturgy have not changed. They have been given to us just as they were given to the first followers of Jesus.

Yet our culture today does influence some aspects of liturgy because our culture expresses our experience of life. The question of change—of what should or should not be changed based on changing culture—is always a very important and serious question for the Church. It is the Church that teaches and guides us in what can be changed and what can never be changed. For example, for two thousand years we have celebrated the Eucharist as the memorial of Christ's death and resurrection. Through sacramental signs we share in this mystery of faith. Bread and wine are transformed into the Body and Blood of Christ. This will never change. The words of institution will never change. How wonderful it is that the Church guides us to this truth and will do so for all time.

CATHOLIC **ID**

The liturgy is a major part of the tradition of the Church. The word *tradition* means "what is handed down." Because the liturgy is handed down to us from the earliest days of the Church, we look to the teaching authority of the Church to guide our liturgical celebration.

But the liturgy is also flexible and open to various cultures. Can you discover unique cultural expressions in African liturgical worship? Latin American? Asian? Magazines from missionary societies may help you with your search.

"The way we pray shows what we believe." Give one example from the liturgy that shows what we believe as Catholics.

What comes to your mind when you say to yourself or someone else, "I'm a Catholic"? Think about the words, feelings, or images the word *Catholic* has for you. Brainstorm with your group. Do these ideas have anything to do with prayer or liturgy? Where does Jesus fit in?

OnLine WITH THE PARISH

The Church is universal, welcoming all peoples and cultures. It might be interesting to discover in your parish or diocese how differing cultural expressions in language, music, and other ways to celebrate are encouraged in the liturgy. One way to experience this might be to join in a liturgy celebrated in a language other than your own. Share your reactions with your group.

YOU ARE MY WITNESSES

Scripture of My Life

The liturgy of the Church has adopted many Jewish liturgical symbols and rituals. Many of these are mentioned in Scripture: praying the psalms as responses; using musical instruments and incense in worship; setting aside one day a week, the Sabbath, as a day of rest and prayer. Among the most important of these practices that we still observe is the reading of the Old Testament in our liturgy. Find the Old Testament reading for this Sunday in a missalette. Read it thoughtfully.

Catholic Teachings

About Liturgy

The liturgy is the most important activity of the Church because it is the work of Christ himself. However, liturgy can never be the *only* activity of the Church. We must believe the good news and live as Jesus' disciples. This means we "love and serve the Lord" by loving and serving others. Liturgy sends us out to serve others, and that experience sends us back to celebrate liturgy. Liturgy and loving service form one unbroken circle.

God's Masterpieces

How great are your works, LORD!

Psalm 92:6

Jesus as the Comforter, August Jerndorff, 1846–1906

Is a sacrament something we pray? something we do? something we receive or something we watch? or something else? What do you think a sacrament is?

God's Master Plan

What is a sacrament? To answer this question, we go back to the very beginning. At the very beginning, when God created the world and everything in it, he had a plan. He did not just create one thing after another without knowing from the very beginning what it would be when it was all finished. The Father had a plan in mind.

Throughout the Old Testament we read about God's plan. Little by little the plan is revealed in the history of his chosen people and through his prophets and messengers. And when the right moment came, this plan was revealed in all its wonderful mystery in the birth, life, passion, death, and resurrection of Jesus Christ. The plan God had in mind was Jesus Christ! In Jesus, God would reveal himself to us most fully. In Jesus, we see God made visible, at once truly human and truly divine.

24

Jesus, the Word Made Flesh

In the first chapters of the Book of Genesis, we glimpse the harmony God plans for the world. Men and women are at peace *with each other*: They are partners and helpers to each other. The human creatures are at peace *with the earth*. They are also at peace *with God*: Adam walks and talks with him in the garden. This is God's plan: He wants all creation to be reconciled and at peace.

Then sin shatters the dream. Peace between human beings dissolves; peace with the earth becomes toil and struggle. And peace with God? When God calls to Adam, Adam hides. He no longer walks and talks freely with God. This is the first sin—the *original* sin. And all of us share in its effects: weakness of will, tendency to sin, suffering, and death.

But God did not give up on the plan. When the time was ripe, God sent his only Son to bring it to fulfillment. This is Jesus, the Word made flesh. Jesus spent his life showing us how to be at peace with one another, with creation, and with his Father and ours. He spent his life teaching love and forgiveness, healing sickness and division. His resurrection and ascension was his victory over death and sin. Jesus is our redeemer. Through him we are saved from sin. His sacrifice on the cross and his victory over sin and death made the Father's plan of peace and harmony possible for us and for our world. The paschal mystery is the promise that God's plan will be fulfilled.

The Son of God, the second Person of the Blessed Trinity, became one of us in Jesus. In Jesus the invisible God becomes visible! In Jesus we see and come to know the invisible God, whom no eye has ever seen.

Think for a moment. How are you at peace with others, with creation, and with God? How can you deepen and strengthen this peace?

The Sacraments

The plan of God did not end with the death of Jesus. After his resurrection, the risen Christ appeared to his apostles and said, "Receive the holy Spirit" (John 20:22). In handing over the Spirit, Jesus handed over to his descendants—his followers, the Church—his own life.

This life of Jesus, this Spirit, dwells now in the Church, in us. The invisible life of God, first made visible in Jesus Christ, is now made visible in the Church. And Jesus has given the Church seven special signs to draw us into union with him and the Father through the power of the Spirit. Through the sacraments we encounter Christ. Through the sacraments we share in the saving work of Jesus Christ our redeemer.

Sacraments are unique signs. They do more than point the way; they *are* the way. For example, the water of Baptism is not only a sign of life. Through the water of Baptism, we truly receive *life*. In the Eucharist the bread and wine are not only signs of the Body and Blood of Christ. They *become* the Body and Blood of Christ.

A sacrament actually brings about—that is, makes real and present—what it signifies. When we celebrate the sacraments, we do not simply celebrate salvation, forgiveness, and union with God. We are in fact saved, forgiven, and made one with Jesus Christ.

A *sacrament* is a visible and effective sign, given to us by Christ, through which we share in God's grace. No wonder that the Church calls the sacraments "God's masterpieces" (*Catechism*, 1091).

Celebrating the Sacraments

The Church celebrates the seven sacraments. In the celebration of each sacrament, four essential qualities are always present.

Ritual Action   A sacrament is God's life in us—grace—expressed in ritual action. Each sacrament has its own symbols and gestures, its own ritual way of expressing the gift of grace being shared. For example, in the sacrament of the Anointing of

the Sick, the sick person is anointed with oil in the sign of the cross. The oil and the cross are signs of the healing given by Christ.

Worship of God   In every sacrament we praise and worship the Holy Trinity in liturgical prayer.

Paschal Mystery   In every sacrament we remember and enter into the paschal mystery and are made part of it in a deeper way.

The Power of the Holy Spirit   The sacraments make the paschal mystery present and effective by the power of the Holy Spirit—by what God does.

 Are sacraments something we only receive? Explain.

God's Plan in Writing

Each of the seven sacraments celebrates some aspect of the plan of God that has come to fulfillment in Christ and in the Church. Sacred Scripture is the written record of this divine plan as it unfolds in history. Sacred Scripture is the inspired word of God. When it is proclaimed, God is speaking to us. So when we Catholics celebrate the liturgy, we hear the word of God.

The proclamation of Sacred Scripture plays a prominent role in every liturgical celebration. In every liturgy we read aloud some part of the story of God's plan. Through the Scriptures we are reminded continually of what God has done for us and what God still plans to do—with our cooperation.

CATHOLIC ID   Because the sacraments are so important, the Church reminds us that the sacramental rites cannot be changed by anyone. Even the supreme authority in the Church can only change the liturgy after faithful reflection and "with religious respect for the mystery of the liturgy" (*Catechism*, 1125).

When we celebrate the liturgy and the sacraments, we celebrate God's plan and our Christian story, which is part of that plan. We need the word of God in the Scriptures to help us to hear our story with faith and understanding and to urge us on to complete the work of Christ in the world. That is why we can say that Catholics are truly people of word and sacrament.

Let us look more closely at the ways the Scriptures are used in our liturgical celebrations.

• The readings and the psalms are from Scripture.

• The prayers and liturgical songs are drawn from Scripture.

• The symbols and rituals in the liturgy take their meaning from Scripture.

In recent times the Church expanded the amount and the variety of the Scripture readings to be proclaimed. These readings are found in an official liturgical book called the *lectionary*.

The *lectionary* contains the Scripture readings assigned to the various days of the Church year. It provides us with a great variety of Scripture readings all through the year. Because it contains the word of God, we treat the lectionary with great respect.

In Every Liturgy

The liturgy of the Church has been influenced by many cultures and many languages. We use important words rooted in Hebrew, Greek, and Latin to explain the meaning behind the rituals and symbols of our liturgy. Some of these important words common to every sacrament are *anamnesis*, *presence*, *doxology*, *epiclesis*, and *berakah*. At first these terms may seem strange. But after we are introduced to them and we see how they function in each of the sacraments, they will begin to seem like old friends.

27

Remembering   As we have already seen, recalling and celebrating the paschal mystery is at the heart of liturgical prayer. The term for this "remembering" is *anamnesis*. This word from the Greek means "memory," as in, "Do this in memory [*anamnesis*] of me." *Anamnesis* is the liturgical act of remembering. This special kind of remembering not only calls to mind a saving act of God that happened in the past but also makes that event present to us now.

When we celebrate the sacraments, we are not merely recalling events that happened long ago and far away. We are celebrating events that are present to us now. What began in the past, in the death and resurrection of Jesus, is continued into the present. *Now* Jesus Christ is risen. *Now* the Holy Spirit comes upon us. And *now* we are sent forth by Christ to love and serve.

Presence   The risen Christ is present and active with us in every sacrament and in every liturgy.

- He is present in the Mass under the signs of bread and wine and in the person of the priest.
- He is present in his power in the sacraments.
- He is present in his word when the Scripture is read.
- He is present in the assembly. Jesus himself said, "Where two or three are gathered together in my name, there am I in the midst of them" (Matthew 18:20).

Glory   Whenever we recall and make present God's plan for us, we experience feelings of thanksgiving and praise, and we give God glory. Each sacrament and liturgical action is a *doxology*, a prayer that gives God glory.

Calling Upon the Holy Spirit   In each sacrament we call upon the Spirit to make us holy and to build up the body of Christ. The technical term for this petition is *epiclesis*. For example, at the Eucharist we ask God:

> Let your Spirit come upon these
>   gifts to make them holy,
> so that they may become for us
> the body ✝ and blood of our Lord,
>   Jesus Christ.

As we explore each of the seven sacraments, look for this prayer of petition, the epiclesis, and see what the prayer asks for. The epiclesis is often the key to understanding the meaning of a sacrament.

Blessing
One of the prayer forms familiar to Jesus and to the early Church was the berakah. The *berakah* is not a specific prayer; rather, it is a prayer *form*. The berakah usually involves three elements: We call on the name of God (invocation). We gratefully remember (anamnesis) all that God has done for us. We make our petition (epiclesis). Here is an example:

> Blessed are you, Lord, God of all
>   creation.
> Through your goodness we have
>   this bread to offer,
> which earth has given and human
>   hands have made.
> It will become for us the bread
>   of life.

This last sentence is really a prayer of petition meaning, "God, make it become for us the bread of life."

 In the prayer above indicate the invocation, anamnesis, and epiclesis.

What is your part in God's plan? How do you think people your age can fulfill it right now? In what way does the Church help you to do this?

OnLine WITH THE PARISH

Understanding the Scriptures has become increasingly important, both for our private prayer and for our celebration of the liturgy. Does your parish provide ways to study the Scripture? Are the Scripture readings for the week listed in the parish bulletin? Is there a Scripture discussion group for young people? If not, think about forming one.

YOU ARE MY WITNESSES

Scripture in My Life

The reading of the Scriptures is an essential part of the celebration of every sacrament. The Church has provided a variety of readings to help us understand the meaning of each sacramental event. Of the readings listed below, which would you choose for these sacraments?

Baptism
John 3:1–6
Matthew 28:18–20

Reconciliation
Micah 6:1–4, 6–8
1 John 4:16–21

Catholic Teachings

About the Sacraments
The whole liturgical life of the Church revolves around the Eucharist and the other sacraments. There are seven sacraments:

- Baptism
- Confirmation
- Eucharist
- Reconciliation
- Anointing of the Sick
- Holy Orders
- Matrimony

Which sacraments have you received?

29

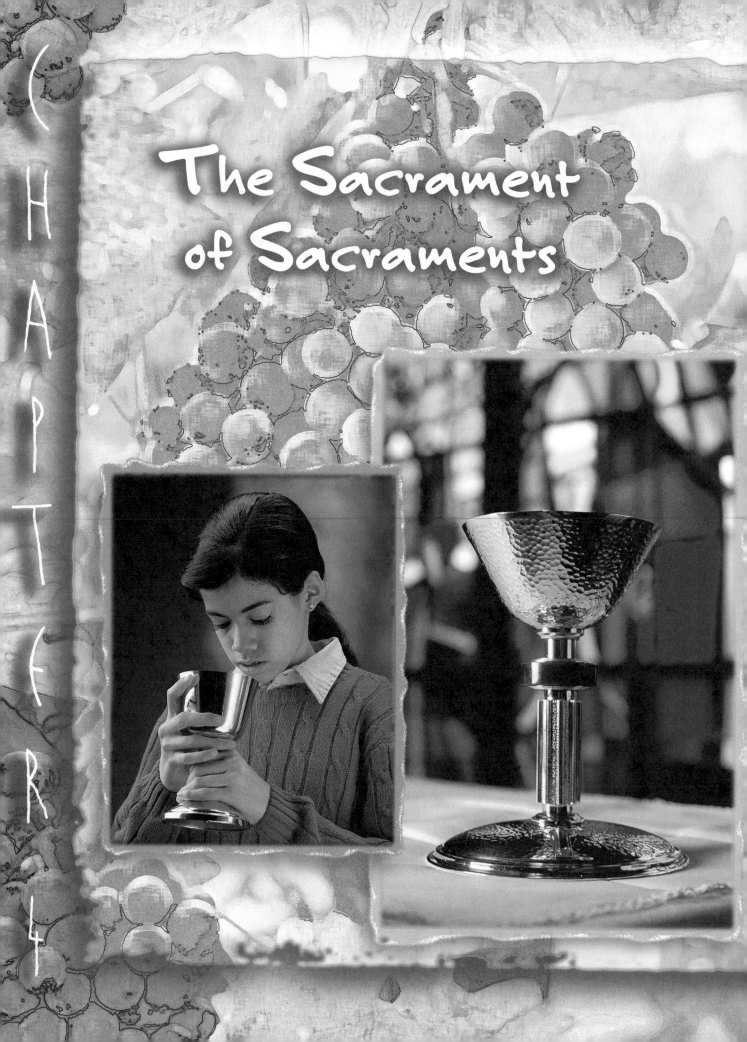

CHAPTER 4

The Sacrament of Sacraments

The cup of blessing that we bless, is it not a participation in the blood of Christ?

The bread that we break, is it not a participation in the body of Christ?

1 Corinthians 10:16

Why is it that we call one sacrament by so many names—Eucharist, the Lord's Supper, the breaking of Bread, the Holy Sacrifice, the sacred mysteries, Holy Communion, and Holy Mass? Why do you think this sacrament is so important?

The Body and Blood of Christ

The Eucharist is the center of our lives. The early Christians knew this. That is why, even under threat of persecution and death, they would risk their lives to come together and celebrate this sacrament. Contemporary Catholics know the same truth. All over the world, whenever and wherever the Mass is celebrated, Catholics will travel for miles or take any risk to be present. Despite any suffering the Church may endure, men and women will always come together as a eucharistic assembly of faith.

What draws people to this sacrament? After all, it has not really changed that much in two thousand years. We still offer the simple gifts of bread and wine. We still gather around the priest who presides at each Mass. Let's take a moment to look more

deeply at this "sacrament of sacraments" that the Church says is the source and summit of our life.

The first thing that Catholics must understand is that the sacrament of the *Eucharist* is really and truly the Body and Blood of Christ. The bread and wine are not just symbols to remind us of Christ. In the Eucharist they have become Christ—body and blood, soul and divinity. Jesus himself told us this. Even before the Last Supper, he said, "I am the living bread that came down from heaven; whoever eats this bread will live forever; and the bread that I will give is my flesh for the life of the world" (John 6:51).

On the night before he died for us, Jesus instituted this sacrament of his Body and Blood. At the Passover feast commemorating God's saving action of bringing the Jewish people from death to life, Jesus took the gifts of unleavened bread and wine and said, "This is my body which will be given up for you. This is the cup of my blood, the blood of the new and everlasting covenant. Do this in memory of me." What had Jesus done? He had given to his Church a living memorial of his saving passion, death, and resurrection. Now, for all time, his disciples could gather together in the presence of their risen Savior and enter into his paschal mystery. They could make themselves part of the one sacrifice of Jesus Christ and give praise to God the Father through him.

How wonderful! How simple and yet full of mystery. The Savior of the world would now be with his Church for all time in a most marvelous way. In this sacred meal the Church would be nourished as the body of Christ by Christ himself. In the liturgy the Church would give thanks—the meaning of Eucharist—for all that God had done through his Son. By the power of the Holy Spirit, the Church would unite itself to Christ by sharing in his Body and Blood.

When we assemble at the Eucharist, we are Christ's body, the Church, and we make this reality visible. We are never more the Church than when we are celebrating the Eucharist around the table of the Lord. In this sacrament of love, our redemption is carried on, we are filled with grace, and a pledge of future glory is given to us (*Catechism*, 1402, 1405).

Our Time, God's Time

Remembering (anamnesis) is at the heart of each of the sacraments. This is especially true of the Eucharist. Every time we celebrate the Eucharist, we hear the words "Do this in memory of me." We remember what Jesus did on Holy Thursday at the Last Supper. We remember what he did for us on Calvary on the first Good Friday. We remember how he rose from the dead on Easter Sunday. Indeed we remember the entire life of Jesus, all that he said and did for us as our redeemer.

When we remember these events at the Eucharist, we do not merely think about events that happened long ago in Jerusalem. The liturgy makes them *present* to us here and now.

How? Imagine that you are looking at a house you have never seen before. If you are standing in front of the house, for example, you see only the front; you can only imagine what the back is like. If you are directly above the house, you have a completely different view, but you still do not see *all* of it. Time is something like that for us. We see only what is before us: the present. We can only read about the past; we can only imagine the future.

For God, however, our past, present, and future are all one. For God all time is *now*. This is a hint of what "God's time of salvation" means. In the liturgy the events we might think of as "past" are actually present. In the liturgy we do not just recall the events of Holy Thursday, Good Friday, and Easter Sunday. These events are made present.

This does not mean that these events are repeated. No. Only the celebrations are repeated. But "in each celebration there is an outpouring of the Holy Spirit that makes the unique mystery present" (*Catechism*, 1104). When we celebrate the liturgy, the mysteries of our faith are made present. We enter into the event. We encounter the presence of Christ, and we are filled with God's grace. When we celebrate the liturgy, we stand in God's time and God's presence.

We must keep in balance the three mysteries—Holy Thursday, Good Friday, and Easter Sunday—and not let any one outweigh the others. A true Catholic understanding of the Eucharist is achieved only when we balance all three. If we think of the Mass as a meal but do not see the relation of the meal to Christ's sacrifice on Good Friday, we do not have a balanced understanding. If we reverence Christ present in the Eucharist but fail to reverence Christ present in the Church (in one another and in the poor), we do not have a balanced understanding of the Eucharist.

We begin with Good Friday in order to understand what we mean when we say the Mass is a *sacrifice*. When we think of sacrifices in the Old Testament,

we might picture the sacrifice of an animal. The blood of the animal was a symbol of life. On the Day of Atonement, the high priest sprinkled this blood on the community. This ritual action was a sign that it was God's own life which gave life to the people. In the life the people now shared with God, their sins were forgiven; they were at one (*at-one*-ment) with God and with one another.

The emphasis in this ritual is not on the killing of the animal but on the celebration of *the people's joyful union with God*. The central meaning of sacrifice, then, is union with God. For the Hebrews, for Jesus, for the early Church, and for us today, *sacrifice* is a ritual action that brings about and celebrates our joyful union with God.

As the early followers of Jesus began to reflect on his death and resurrection, they began to understand the Good Friday event as a sacrifice. Jesus began to be seen as the Lamb of God, the paschal victim—slain, yes, but victorious in the end. Jesus broke the chains of death. Through his sacrifice our sins were forgiven and we were reunited with God. Only Jesus, the spotless victim, could have done this.

We believe that the celebration of the Eucharist makes present to us the sacrifice Jesus offered once and for all on the cross. At the Eucharist we remember Good Friday not merely as an event from the past. The sacrifice of Jesus is a *mystery*; it is more than words can say. It is a mystery we remember and make present each time we celebrate the Eucharist.

 Have you ever made a sacrifice that gave life, even in a small way?

The Eucharistic Prayer

At each Eucharist we hear these or similar words:

> While they were at supper,
> he took bread, said the blessing, broke the bread,
> and gave it to his disciples, saying:
> Take this, all of you, and eat it:
> this is my body which will be given up for you.

What a wonderful phrase to reflect on: "my body which will be given up for you." In joining with

Crucifixion, Sadao Watanabe, 1970

Christ to celebrate this Holy Thursday meal, we celebrate and make present the sacrifice of Good Friday. Sacrifices are celebrated in many different ways. One form of sacrifice known to Jesus and the early Church was the sacred meal: Eating and drinking together symbolized and brought about joyful union with God.

Today, at the Holy Sacrifice of the Mass, the meal is the external sign of the sacrifice. We do not ask whether the Mass is a sacrifice *or* a meal; it is *both*. The sharing of food and drink, the meal itself, is the sacrament. It is the external sign of the sacrifice. What we *see* is a meal; what the meal *makes present* is the sacrifice.

Before meals most Catholics "say grace." They say a prayer thanking God for the food they are about to eat and asking God to bless them as they share their meal. At the Eucharist, the greatest of all meals, we say, through the priest, the eucharistic prayer, the greatest of all meal prayers.

The basic shape of this meal prayer is that of the prayer of blessing (berakah) known to Jesus and the apostles. In this prayer:

- We call upon the name of God (invocation).
- We gratefully remember all that God has done for us (anamnesis).
- We make our petition (epiclesis).

The eucharistic prayer begins with a dialogue between the priest and the people, "The Lord be with you. . . . Lift up your hearts. . . ." Then we call on God, our loving Father, and give thanks for all the wonderful things he has done for us. We thank God most especially for Jesus. We remember what Jesus did for us at the Last Supper; we remember his passion, death, and resurrection. And we make our petition. We ask God to send the Holy Spirit to change the bread and wine into the Body and Blood of Christ. We ask that we who eat the Bread and drink the Cup may become one body in that same Spirit.

When we listen closely to the words of the eucharistic prayer and understand the meaning of this greatest "grace before meals," we understand the relationship between Holy Thursday and the meaning of the Eucharist.

In order to understand the Eucharist well, we must hold these images of Good Friday and Holy Thursday in their proper balance. And to these two we add a third: the image of Easter Sunday.

 Find a song about the Eucharist in a hymnal or a missalette. What does it say about a meal? a sacrifice?

We Are One Body

Jesus told us, "I am with you always, until the end of the age" (Matthew 28:20). The Eucharist is the celebration of this abiding presence of Jesus in our midst. The risen Jesus makes us one with him in the Church. Through Baptism, Confirmation, and Eucharist, we have become the body of Christ.

 CATHOLIC ID The words that Catholics use reflect what they believe about the Eucharist. Out of deep respect for Christ's real presence in the Eucharist, we call the consecrated Bread the *Host*, and the consecrated Wine the *Precious Blood*.

Supper at Emmaus, Ivo Dulčič, 1916

This is the heart of Easter Sunday: Christ is totally identified with us, his followers, his Church. Our work now is to be the presence of Christ in the world.

This is what Paul the Apostle, once called Saul, learned on the road to Damascus. In the Acts of the Apostles we see Saul on his way to persecute the followers of Jesus. Suddenly, "he fell to the ground and heard a voice saying to him, 'Saul, Saul, why are you persecuting me?' He said, 'Who are you, sir?' The reply came, 'I am Jesus, whom you are persecuting'" (Acts 9:4–5).

This experience taught Paul that Christ cannot be separated from his members. The risen Lord is so united to us, his followers, that what we do to one another we do to Christ. This fact is central to our understanding of the real presence of Christ at the Eucharist. Paul met Christ who was so identified with us that to persecute Christians was to persecute Christ himself.

Around A.D. 50, Paul wrote to the Corinthians regarding some concerns he had about the way they were celebrating the Eucharist. At issue was their understanding of the presence of Christ in the Eucharist. Paul had heard of the divisions between the rich and the poor that separated the community.

The poor are going hungry while the rich eat and drink all they want. Paul scolds the Corinthians for celebrating the Eucharist without recognizing the body of Christ— his Church. He tells them that this is the "body of Christ" they must see at the Eucharist if they are to celebrate worthily. He reminds them that all who eat and drink without recognizing *this* body eat and drink judgment on themselves. Sharing the Eucharist is a promise that we will treat all people as Christ would treat them—indeed, as we would treat Christ himself. This is also what it means to "do this in memory of me."

So the next time you hear the words "Body of Christ" at Communion remember and believe that:
• Christ is really and truly present in the Eucharist.
• We the Church are the body of Christ.

If we believe these things about the Eucharist, then the words of Saint Augustine can both make sense to us and challenge us: "We become what we eat"—that is, in the Eucharist we can be transformed into Christ.

Why do you think it is so important to prepare to receive Christ in the Eucharist and to receive him worthily?

Things to SHARE

The next time you go to Mass, will the images of Holy Thursday, Good Friday, and Easter Sunday play a part in your thoughts and prayers? Will you picture yourself at table with Jesus? How can you be more aware of those around you and of the ways that together you form the body of Christ? How will the poor and those in need fit into your celebration? Write your thoughts in your journal.

OnLine WITH THE PARISH

Each parish church reflects an understanding of the Eucharist celebrated there. Look around your parish church to see which furnishings and decorations emphasize Holy Thursday, Good Friday, and Easter Sunday. Is there a large crucifix over the altar, or is there an image of the risen Christ? Do you think the altar/table looks more like an altar for sacrifice or like a table for a meal? Does it look like both?

YOU ARE MY WITNESSES

Scripture of My Life

In their gospels Matthew, Mark, and Luke describe the supper Jesus celebrated with his disciples on the night before he died. Each tells how Jesus took bread and wine, gave it to the disciples, and said, "This is my body; this is my blood."

These important words of Jesus do not appear in John's Gospel. Instead we read how Jesus "poured water into a basin and began to wash the disciples' feet" (John 13:5). What does Jesus say this action means? (See John 13:12–20.) What do you think Jesus' gesture tells us about the Eucharist?

Catholic Teachings

About the Eucharist

During the eucharistic prayer, the bread and wine are transformed. They become the Body and Blood of Christ. How does this happen?

What the bread and wine really are—their substance—becomes the Body and Blood of Christ. Their appearances—what they look and taste like—do not change.

The substance is changed into Christ while the appearances remain the same. This change is called *transubstantiation*.

37

CHAPTER 5

Celebrating Eucharist

He was made known to them
in the breaking of the bread.

Luke 24:35

What would you say if a friend who had
never been to Mass asked you,
"What do you Catholics do when you
go to church on Sunday?"

Owning the Eucharist

Most of us have been celebrating the Eucharist almost all our lives, so we may think we know it well. But the Eucharist is a great mystery, so there is always more to understand, more to appreciate, more to celebrate. The Eucharist is a community action, a liturgical action. It requires the participation of each and every one of us, the entire body of Christ.

"Doing" is different from just "watching." Doing requires information and skills. Playing the trumpet in the band requires more information and skills than watching the parade go by. At the Eucharist we are the "players"; we *all* celebrate the Eucharist together. We each have an active part, whether that be reading, listening, bringing up the gifts, singing, or responding together with our "Amen!" In the last chapter we studied what the Eucharist means. Now we want to learn how to celebrate that meaning.

The external shape of the Mass is a meal. It will help us understand how to celebrate the Eucharist if we first think of what we do when we celebrate a special meal in our homes. For example, how might you celebrate Thanksgiving dinner at your grandmother's house?

Each person's Thanksgiving might be a little different, but we would probably find these same four parts in any meal of celebration: (1) We gather. (2) We tell our stories. (3) We share our meal by putting food on the table, saying the blessing, and eating and drinking. (4) We return home.

The Eucharistic meal has a similar four-fold structure:
- gathering
- storytelling
- meal sharing: preparation of the gifts, the eucharistic prayer, the communion rite
- commissioning.

Each of these elements has its own special purpose. The better we understand each of these four parts of the Eucharist, the better will we be able to celebrate the Eucharist with meaning.

Gathering

We come together in one place for the eucharistic assembly. We gather together as the Church to make the body of Christ visible.

The priest invites us to make the sign of the cross. He greets us, saying "The Lord be with you." We respond, "And also with you." This greeting is used

several times during the Mass. It is intended both as a wish, meaning "*May* the Lord be with you" and as a profound statement of faith, meaning "As you assemble for worship, the Lord *is* with you." The Introductory Rites are intended *to gather us together into a worshiping assembly*. We are asked to pause and recall our common need for salvation (the penitential rite). On Sundays and feasts, we sing or recite the hymn "Glory to God in the highest." At the close of the Introductory Rites that gather us together, the priest asks us to join our hearts and minds in prayer. After a few moments of silence, the priest "collects" our intentions into one prayer. We make it our own by responding "Amen."

Storytelling

When we gather for a meal, we usually begin with conversation: telling our stories. At the Eucharist, after the Introductory Rites, we sit down and enter into the ritual of conversation with Sacred Scripture, the inspired word of God. We do this in the Liturgy of the Word.

Through the reading of the Scriptures, we listen to the Father's story once again. On Sundays we have three opportunities, because there are three readings. The first reading is ordinarily taken from the Old Testament and is related in theme to the gospel of the day. This Old Testament reading recalls, in some way, God the Father's original covenant with us.

Preparation of the Gifts

The Dialogue

Following the first reading we sing or recite a psalm, a song from the Book of Psalms. The second reading is usually from one of the letters of Paul or from another apostolic writing. The first two readings conclude with "The word of the Lord." To this we all respond with our liturgical "yes" as we say, "Thanks be to God."

The third reading is taken from one of the four gospels. Because of the unique respect given to the gospel words of Jesus, it has long been the custom in the Church to stand in attentive reverence during the proclamation of the gospel.

Before proclaiming the gospel, the priest greets us with "The Lord be with you." As he announces the particular gospel of the day, he traces with his right thumb a series of three small crosses on his forehead, on his lips, and on his heart. Silently he prays that God will cleanse his mind and his heart so that his lips may proclaim the gospel worthily. In many places the congregation makes these small signs of the cross along with the priest. The gospel reading concludes with, "The gospel of the Lord." We respond, "Praise to you, Lord Jesus Christ." We thus proclaim our faith in the presence of Christ in the word. Then we sit for the homily.

The *homily* takes the word of God and brings it to our life today. Just as a large piece of bread must be broken to be eaten, a good homily "breaks open" the word of God in order that we might hear, understand, and act upon it.

On Sundays we then stand and together recite the Nicene Creed.

The creed is a statement of our faith in the word we have heard proclaimed in the Scripture and the homily. The creed reminds us of the faith we accepted at Baptism. As we make our profession of faith at Mass, we are reminded that each time we come to the Eucharist, we come through Baptism.

General Intercessions   The Liturgy of the Word comes to a close with what are called the general intercessions.

In the general intercessions, we pray that our Church and our world might come to look like the plan God has for us. Our petitions usually fall into four categories: the needs of the universal Church, all nations and their leaders, people in special need, and the needs of our local parish. As these petitions are announced, we all pray for these intentions in our hearts. Then we make our common response aloud: "Lord, hear our prayer."

What will you pray for so that your parish community will "reflect" the body of Christ proclaimed in the Scripture?

Epiclesis

Consecration and Anamnesis

Doxology

Following the Liturgy of the Word, we move to the table of the Lord. In any meal celebration there are three movements: We bring the food to the table, say grace, and share the food. At Mass these actions are called the preparation of the gifts, the eucharistic prayer, and the communion rite.

Preparation of the Gifts   Members of the community bring the bread and wine for the Eucharist to the priest at the altar. Then begins the preparation of gifts. The priest places the bread and wine on the table. He mixes water with wine and washes his hands. These gestures remind us of the Last Supper: Mixing water with the wine and washing hands were rituals the Jews followed at all meals in Jesus' time. The priest then invites us to pray that our sacrifice be acceptable to God. We respond "Amen" to the prayer over the gifts and stand to participate in the central prayer of the Mass.

The Eucharistic Prayer

The eucharistic prayer brings us to the very center of the Mass and to the heart of our Catholic faith. The structure of this prayer is that of a berakah.

The Dialogue   The eucharistic prayer begins with a dialogue between the priest and the assembly: "The Lord be with you. . . ." The priest then asks if we are ready and willing to approach the table, to renew our baptismal commitment, to offer ourselves to God: "Lift up your hearts." And we say: "We lift them up to the Lord." The priest invites us to give thanks to the Lord our God. And we respond: "It is right to give him thanks and praise." (The word *eucharist* comes from the Greek, "to give thanks and praise.")

The Preface   The priest begins the preface. Here *preface* retains its original meaning of speaking in the presence of God. We are brought into God's presence and speak directly to God, thanking him for his wonderful works. We join the choirs of angels, who praise God unendingly in the heavenly liturgy, saying:

> Holy, holy, holy Lord, God of power and might, heaven and earth are full of your glory.

Epiclesis   The priest invokes the Father (epiclesis) to send the Holy Spirit to change our gifts of bread and wine into the Body and Blood of Christ. We also pray that we who take part in this Eucharist may become one body and one spirit. Only then can we experience the fullest presence of Christ.

Anamnesis   The priest recalls the events of the Last Supper and the story of the institution of the Eucharist. (These words are called the "words of consecration.")

CATHOLIC **ID**

Do you know that we Catholics consider the Eucharist a sacrament of reconciliation? The Church tells us that when we receive the Eucharist worthily, our venial sins are forgiven. The Eucharist strengthens our love for God, self, and others, and this love wipes out sin. The Eucharist also preserves us from future sin. "The more we share the life of Christ and progress in his friendship, the more difficult it is to break away from him" (*Catechism*, 1395). Forgiveness of sin springs from the principal effect of the Eucharist in our lives: union with Christ.

He then speaks to us, inviting us to "proclaim the mystery of faith." A short and familiar acclamation is:

Christ has died,
Christ is risen,
Christ will come again.

The priest continues to recall with us (anamnesis) the wonderful deeds which saved us: the passion, death, and resurrection of Christ.

Epiclesis for Unity The grateful memory of God's salvation leads us to make the second half of our petition—our primary petition (epiclesis) at every Eucharist—the petition for unity. We look forward to that glorious feast of never-ending joy in heaven and join our voices with those of all the saints who have gone before us as the priest raises the bread and wine and offers a doxology, a prayer of glory to God in the name of Christ:

Through him,
with him,
in him,
in the unity of the Holy Spirit,
all glory and honor is yours,
almighty Father,
for ever and ever.

Our "Amen" to this prayer acclaims our assent and participation in the entire eucharistic prayer.

 Look back at the parts of the eucharistic prayer on these pages. What do you think we are saying "yes" to in each of the parts?

The Communion Rite

Now, we prepare to eat and drink at the Lord's table by praying together the Lord's Prayer: "Give us this day our daily bread; and forgive us our trespasses as we forgive those who trespass against us."

Communion is the sign and source of our reconciliation and union with God and with one another. Therefore, we make a gesture of union and forgiveness with those around us and offer them a sign of peace.

The priest then shows us the Bread and Cup and invites us to come to the table:

This is the Lamb of God. . . .
Happy are those who are called to his supper.

Here we are once more reminded that the Mass is both a sacrifice and a meal. We come forward to eat and drink the Body and Blood of Christ. We approach the minister, who gives us the eucharistic Bread with the words "The body of Christ." We respond "Amen." We then go to the minister with the Cup who offers it to us with the words "The blood of Christ," to which we again profess our "Amen."

During this procession we usually sing a hymn which unites our voices, thoughts, and spirits, even as the Body and Blood of Christ unites us as one body in Christ. Then we pray silently in our hearts, asking for all that this sacrament promises. The priest unites our prayers in the prayer after Communion, to which we respond "Amen."

Commissioning

Finally we prepare to go back to that world in which we work and play, study and live. The burdens we have laid down at the door of the church for this Eucharist we now take up again. But now we bear them with the strength received from this Eucharist and this community. The priest again says "The Lord be with you," this ritual phrase serving now as a farewell.

We bow our heads to receive a blessing. As the priest blesses us in the name of the Trinity, we make the sign of the cross as we did at the beginning of the Mass. The priest or deacon then dismisses the assembly: "Go in peace to love and serve the Lord." And we give our liturgical "yes" as we say "Thanks be to God."

 Reflect for a moment. Decide on one way you will go forth from the Eucharist to be "bread" for someone.

With several of your friends, recall a time when you really enjoyed celebrating a liturgy—when it was especially meaningful for you. As you tell your story and listen to the stories of your friends, ask what it was about these liturgies that made them "good." How do the things that make liturgy a good experience relate to the things which we have studied in this chapter?

OnLine WITH THE PARISH

Does your parish need readers, singers, ushers, or altar servers? Sacristans (those who help prepare the altar for Mass) may be needed, too. Volunteer your help. Often parishes offer training sessions for these ministries. Does yours? When we each do our part well, we help the whole parish to celebrate the Eucharist together in the best possible way.

YOU ARE MY WITNESSES

Scripture of My Life

In Luke's Gospel we read the story of two disciples on the road to Emmaus. This story is the source of the fourfold structure we are using to understand the Mass. Read Luke 24:13–35 in your Bible. See if you can identify the four movements:

• Who gathers?

• What stories do they tell?

• Where do they recognize the presence of the risen Lord?

• What do they do at the end of the story, "after Mass"?

CATHOLIC TEACHINGS

About the Mass

It is Christ himself, acting through the ministry of priests, who offers the eucharistic sacrifice. Only validly ordained priests can preside at the Eucharist and consecrate the bread and wine. Through Baptism, however, all of us share in the priesthood of Christ. This is called "the common priesthood of the faithful." Laypeople may take on special roles in the liturgy, serving as readers, altar servers, and eucharistic ministers.

The Sacraments
of Initiation

I am the light of the world.
Whoever follows me will not walk in
darkness, but will have the light of life.

John 8:12

Think about one new beginning you
might already have made in your life.
Was it hard? Did you have help?
Has it made your life better?
What beginnings are you
looking forward to?

Beginnings

How do you begin to become a Catholic? This probably doesn't seem to be a very important question if you already are a Catholic! Many of us were baptized when we were infants and have been Catholics ever since. In fact, since the earliest times, Baptism has been administered to infants and children. This continues today. But even so, the question of becoming Catholic is very important. That is because the *process* by which an unbaptized person becomes a Catholic is like a map that helps us understand how to follow Jesus.

The Church realizes that people coming to the Catholic faith as adults need a different kind of preparation, the kind that the early Church gave to the first converts from paganism. This preparation is called the *Rite of Christian Initiation of Adults* (*RCIA*). Through the liturgies and prayers it provides, the RCIA prepares adults and young people to become members of the Catholic Church. Sometimes this preparation can last one or two years. New Catholics are initiated into the Church by receiving the three *sacraments of initiation*—Baptism, Confirmation, and Eucharist—all at once, usually at the Easter Vigil. So understanding the RCIA is a good way to understand the three sacraments of initiation.

Eucharist is closely connected to Baptism and Confirmation. Every time we come to the Eucharist, we come "through Baptism." (This is why we dip our fingers into the baptismal water and make the sign of the cross when we enter a church.) At each Eucharist we renew the promises of our Baptism: the promises to renounce evil and to follow Christ.

In order to understand our baptismal promises, we first need to learn about conversion. *Conversion* is the process of coming to believe that Jesus Christ is the Savior of the world. The word literally means "turning around, going in the other direction."

If conversion is a turning around, what do we *turn from*? What do we *turn toward*? Saint Paul tells us

we are to *turn from* the flesh, all that is selfish, all that seeks "me first" without considering what God wants, all that is sinful. We are to *turn toward* the spiritual, all that is life-giving and selfless, all that is generous, all that is filled with the Holy Spirit. Conversion is a lifelong task. Baptism is our first "turning," or act of conversion, but this process continues throughout our lives. It is made possible by the paschal mystery of Jesus Christ.

Becoming a Catholic

When an unbaptized person wants to become a Catholic or to see what the Catholic Church is all about, he or she usually seeks out a parish and participates in a series of inquiry evenings or information sessions. In some cases, moved by the grace of the Holy Spirit, the person might decide to take the first formal steps toward becoming a Catholic. This is called becoming a catechumen, or entering the catechumenate. The catechumenate

has four parts: instruction, moral conversion, worship, and ministry.

The root meaning of *catechumenate* is instruction. *Instruction* is the first step, an important part of the catechumenate. A person who wants to become a Catholic will naturally want to know what Catholics know. Above all, a catechumen must know Jesus and his Church.

The second step along the journey is "changing one's way of life," or *moral conversion*. As we come to know Jesus, we will want to act like Jesus. We will want to convert, "to turn around" and follow Jesus.

Worship is the third step along the way. Part of becoming a Catholic is worshiping together with Catholics, praying in a Catholic way. Catechumens will usually participate in Sunday Mass. They will leave after the homily in order to continue their reflection on the word of God while the baptized community celebrates the Eucharist.

49

Rite of Acceptance into the Order of Catechumens: presenting the gospels

Until they are baptized, catechumens are not able to participate fully in the Eucharist.

The fourth step is *ministry*. Those who know Jesus will want to tell others about Jesus. They will want to share their faith and serve others in his name.

Have you ever felt called to conversion, to changing your way of life? What did you do about it?

Initiation

There comes a day when a catechumen decides to ask for the sacraments of initiation: Baptism, Confirmation, and Eucharist. Because the catechumen chooses or elects the Church and the Church chooses or elects the individual, the catechumens are now called the elect. The *Rite of Election* takes place on the first Sunday of Lent.

The season of Lent is a season of spiritual retreat during which the

Rite of Election

catechumens prepare for their reception of Baptism, Confirmation, and Eucharist at the Easter Vigil. It is a time for those who are already baptized to encourage the catechumens, and to pray with them. At the Easter Vigil, the Saturday night before Easter, all that the catechumens have been preparing for comes together.

A *vigil* is a time to wait and watch. The liturgy begins after nightfall. We gather around the Easter fire and listen to Scriptures that call to mind the wonder of our salvation. We shout forth our alleluia, which is fresh and new because we have not used it during the forty days of Lent. And we hear in the gospel the proclamation that Jesus has risen from the dead.

Then the elect come forward. They go down into the baptismal water, down into the tomb with Jesus: They are baptized. They emerge from the baptismal pool dripping wet with new life. The newly baptized are then clothed with a white

Easter Vigil

garment, symbolizing that they have "clothed [themselves] with Christ" (Galatians 3:27). They are given candles lit from the Easter candle. Then they are anointed with oil: They are confirmed.

The vigil comes to its climax with the celebration of the Eucharist. The newly initiated join us for the first time at the table of the Lord.

Baptism

In the New Testament Christian initiation is described by means of many symbols and images. Baptism is "being born again." In this sacrament we come forth from the waters of Baptism and are born into God's family. We are filled with the Spirit of love, welcomed by the Christian community, and receive the family name "Christian." We start afresh. All our sins—original sin and all personal sins—are taken away.

Baptism is also a "dying." In Baptism we go down into the tomb, and are buried with Christ. We die to selfishness and sin so that the Spirit of Christ might be born in us.

Baptism is "seeing things in a new light." We emerge from the waters of Baptism and see things with God's eyes. We see a world in which we are no longer alone, a world in which we are connected with every other creature. We see a world in which we are loved and given power by the Spirit of God.

Baptism is "being adopted into a new family," the family of God. As family members we are brothers and sisters of Jesus Christ. We inherit everything that God has given to his Son, especially the great gift of eternal life.

Through these baptismal images the Church teaches that "Baptism is the basis of the whole Christian life, the gateway to life in the Spirit . . . and the door which gives access to the other sacraments" (*Catechism*, 1213). Through Baptism we are made members of Christ and members of his body, the Church. We are in Christ and Christ is in us. His work, his mission in the world, is now our own.

 Which image of Baptism has greatest meaning for you? Why?

Celebrating Baptism

We have learned that the principal prayer of each sacrament is often expressed as a prayer of blessing (berakah): (1) We call God by name, "Father." (2) We gratefully remember what God has done for us. (3) We invoke the Holy Spirit.

At Baptism the blessing of the water takes this form. The priest moves to the water and calls upon God. He prays that the Father will give us grace through the sign of the gift of water. As the prayer continues, we remember (anamnesis) God's saving acts, especially those involving water. We pray that all who are buried with Christ in Baptism may rise with him to new life.

The candidates are plunged into this water three times (or water is poured over their heads three times), and the priest baptizes them in the name of the Father, and of the Son, and of the Holy Spirit. The newly baptized come up from the water risen with Christ and all is now new.

Confirmation

At the Easter Vigil the sacraments of initiation are celebrated together in one liturgy. The meaning of each of the three sacraments is found in the meaning of the other two and in the meaning of the whole ceremony. Catholics who were baptized as infants receive Confirmation later, usually at a time when they can understand what the sacrament means.

CATHOLIC ID The ordinary minister of Baptism is a bishop, priest, or deacon. But did you know that in case of necessity, anyone can baptize? In an emergency a person baptizes by pouring water over the head of the one to be baptized while saying, "I baptize you in the name of the Father, and of the Son, and of the Holy Spirit."

We do not find many writings about Confirmation dating from the early days of the Church because it was thought of as part of Baptism. When they spoke of Baptism, the early Christians meant Baptism-Confirmation.

Baptism washes away sin and frees us from original sin. *Original sin* was the rejection of God by our first parents, resulting in the loss of sanctifying grace. With their sin, Adam and Eve deprived themselves and all their descendants of the original state of grace given by God. Because of original sin, we need to be saved by Jesus and restored to God's grace.

Baptism washes away original sin and fills us with God's own life through the power of the Holy Spirit. This is what we call *sanctifying grace*. In God, the source of all holiness, we share in holiness. Confirmation seals us with the Spirit, strengthening the grace of Baptism. Baptism changes us so radically that we can never be "unbaptized." Baptism makes us members of Christ's body, and this can never be undone. It is an indelible spiritual mark, or character, that cannot be taken away.

Confirmation strengthens and continues our Baptism. We receive the Holy Spirit in a special way. We are incorporated more firmly into Christ. Like Baptism, Confirmation marks us with an indelible character. The sacrament never needs to be repeated—nor can it be.

Celebrating Confirmation

A good way to understand Confirmation is to look at the way the Church celebrates it. First, the bishop or the delegated priest extends his hands over you (the typical gesture of invoking the Holy Spirit). Then, as he lays his hand on your head, he anoints your forehead with oil (remember that the name *Christ* means the "anointed one") and says, "Be sealed with the Gift of the Holy Spirit."

In Confirmation we are anointed with oil. It is a sign of consecration. We are anointed in order to share more fully in the mission of Jesus Christ. We are anointed as a sign that we have the seal of the Holy Spirit. Now we belong totally to Christ; we are enrolled in his service forever.

Things to SHARE

We have seen that conversion is an ongoing process. Each day we continue to turn from all that is selfish and to turn toward all that is Spirit-filled and life-giving.

Can you name objects or activities in the life of a person your age that would be selfish in this context? Can you name objects or activities that are Spirit-filled?

OnLine WITH THE PARISH

When are Baptisms scheduled in your parish? Are infants baptized during Sunday Mass? See if you can find out.

Sometimes the names of new Catholics are printed in the parish bulletin. Can you think of a way to make them feel welcome? You may wish to invite them to a prayer service on the theme of the sacraments of initiation.

YOU ARE MY WITNESSES

Scripture My Life

Very often during the rite of Confirmation, you may hear these words of Jesus about the Holy Spirit: "The Advocate, the holy Spirit that the Father will send in my name— he will teach you everything" (John 14:26). Here are a few more Scriptures from the rite of Confirmation. What do they say about the Holy Spirit in your life?

Luke 4:16–22   John 7:37–39

Catholic Teachings

About Baptism

Sometimes people may worry about others who die without being baptized. The Church teaches that those who have not been baptized but who die for the faith receive the grace of Baptism by their martyrdom. This is called the *Baptism of blood.* Unbaptized people who die, if they are catechumens or people who have sincerely tried to do the will of God, even without knowing the Church, are saved by what is called the *Baptism of desire.*

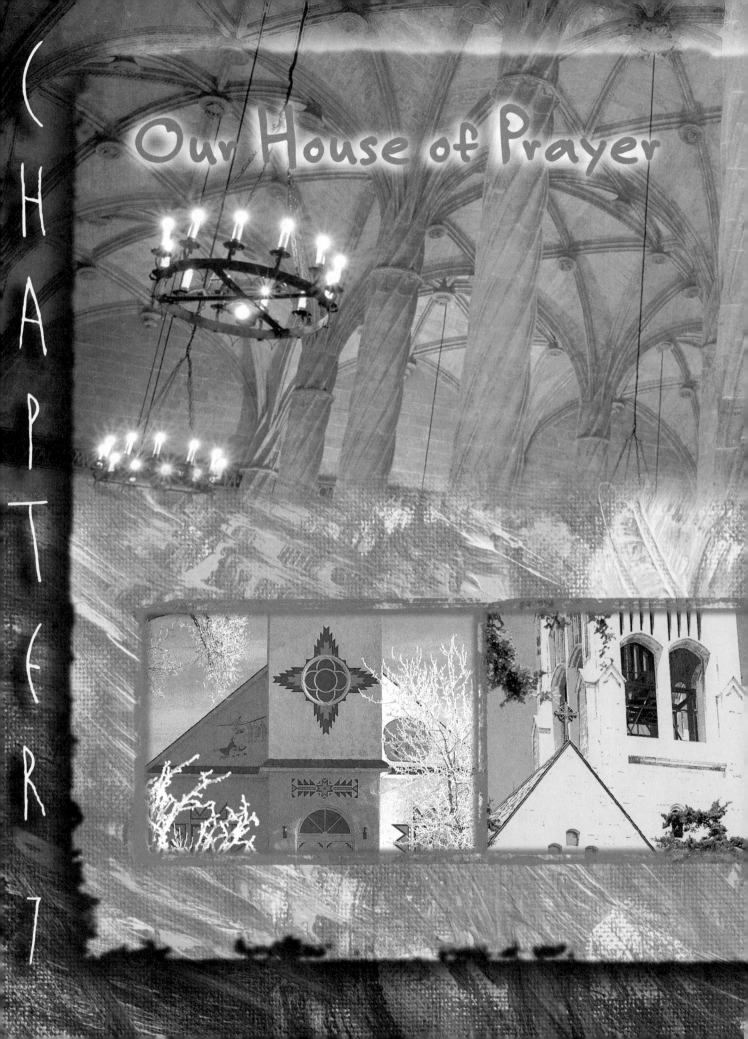

CHAPTER 7

Our House of Prayer

LORD, I love the house where you dwell,
the tenting-place of your glory.

Psalm 26:8

55

You might sometimes hear people say,
"I don't need a church. I can worship God anywhere."
It is true that God can be found and worshiped anywhere.
Why is a sacred place, a church, so important to us?

A Temple of Living Stones

Jesus himself needed and respected sacred space. He often found his own sacred space in "a deserted place" (Mark 1:35) where he prayed quietly alone. But he also gathered in places of worship with others. At the age of twelve, he went on pilgrimage with his parents to the Temple in Jerusalem (Luke 2:41). As an adult he prayed in the synagogue on the Sabbath "according to his custom" (Luke 4:16) and at least once even took a leading part in worship by reading the Scriptures (Luke 4:17). He often taught in the Temple and was concerned that the Temple truly be a house of prayer, not a marketplace (Luke 19:45–46).

Jesus taught something new about worship. Once a Samaritan woman asked him where it was best to worship—on the mountain where her ancestors had prayed or in Jerusalem. Jesus replied, "The hour is coming when you will worship the Father neither on this mountain nor in Jerusalem. . . . God is Spirit, and those who worship him must worship in Spirit and truth" (John 4:21–24).

What does this mean? It means that we now worship God in the Spirit and truth of Jesus, the Son of God. Although we do need places to worship, Jesus tells us that he himself is the primary place, the temple where God dwells. Through the sacraments of initiation, we are incorporated into this new temple, this body of Christ. We are now the sign and sacrament of God's presence on earth.

Our worship of God in the body of Christ, in the Spirit and truth of Jesus, "is not tied exclusively to any one place. The whole earth is sacred" (*Catechism*, 1179). In this sense it is true that we do not need church buildings. But this is not the whole story.

After Jesus ascended into heaven, his disciples would gather on the first day of the week to keep his message alive and to celebrate his risen presence in the Eucharist. They needed a *place* to do this: a place to come together, to tell their stories, and to share their meal.

At first the early Christians met in one another's homes. Later, when assemblies grew larger and worship in public became more acceptable, they used Roman basilicas for their gatherings. A *basilica* was not a temple or a place of worship; rather, it was a building designed for public meetings and other business. Even later, when Christians began to design and build their own churches, they used the familiar basilica form as a model, often adapting it to the shape of a cross.

The House of God

Our parish church, the place where we gather to worship, is a visible sign of our faith. It is the place where God dwells, the tenting place of his eucharistic presence. It is not only a house for us, for the Church, but also God's house. "Behold, God's dwelling is with the human race. He will dwell with them and they will be his people and God himself will always be with them" (Revelation 21:3).

A Place of Celebration

Our parish church serves multiple purposes, but the most important is the celebration of the Eucharist. How does the church building itself help us to celebrate the Eucharist?

Gathering The church is the place where we gather together for worship. This fact makes the design of a church different from the design of a sports stadium or a movie theater, for example. Most large public spaces have a stage where the action takes place and an area set aside for the spectators or audience. In church there is no stage because at Mass there is no audience. We are all *doers*, and the entire assembly area is the stage.

From wherever we stand in the assembly area, our attention is drawn to three important objects: the presider's chair, the lectern, and the altar. The presider's chair is positioned so that the priest is seen to be both a member of the assembly and the leader of the assembly. In the principal church of a diocese, the chair (*cathedra* in Latin) for the bishop gives its name to the entire building, the *cathedral*.

Chancery Chapel, Diocese of Victoria (Texas)

St. Mary's Cathedral, San Francisco

Storytelling   The church must be designed for the proclamation of God's word. We must be able to hear and see well. Good acoustics (sound quality) and sight lines are very important for this function.

The readings are proclaimed from the *lectern*, or *ambo*, a reading stand upon which the lectionary is placed and from which we proclaim the word of God.

Meal Sharing   As the liturgical action moves from storytelling to the sharing of our meal, our attention moves from the lectern to the altar. The altar is not an ordinary table. On the *altar* the sacrifice of the cross is made present under the sacramental signs. The altar is also the table of the Lord, to which we are all invited.

The altar, which is anointed with oil when a church is dedicated, also represents Christ, the Anointed One. As a sign of love for Christ, the priest greets the altar with an act of reverence at the beginning and end of the Eucharist.

In the thirteenth century Catholics did not receive Holy Communion frequently. Instead, looking at the sacred Host after the consecration became the high point of the Mass. So Catholics began to kneel during the eucharistic prayer. As the practice of kneeling was extended, kneeling benches were added.

Commissioning   Following Communion we are dismissed and commissioned to take the gospel message from the church to our daily lives in the world. What happens in the church must be connected to our lives outside the church. This connection is made clearer when the design and furnishings of the church building are related to the community it serves.

58

A Place of Worship

Because the sacrament of Baptism is the spiritual door to the Church, the baptismal font or baptismal pool is located near the front door whenever possible. In fact one early Church custom was to build the baptismal pool completely outside the church, in a separate building near the entrance. This building was called the *baptistry*. It signified the absolute need for Baptism before celebrating the Eucharist with the assembly. Today as we enter the doors of the church, we dip our fingers into blessed water and make the sign of the cross, that sign in which we were baptized. Each time we gather as the body of Christ for Eucharist, we continue and renew the celebration of our Baptism.

In this baptismal area you will also see a niche in the wall or a little chest called the *ambry*. It contains three vessels of oil: the oil of catechumens, which is used to bless and strengthen those preparing for baptism; the oil of the sick, with which the priest strengthens and heals those who are ill; and the sacred chrism, which is used in celebrating the sacraments of Baptism, Confirmation, and Holy Orders. The word *Christ* means "anointed one." So being anointed with oil is a sign of the special and strengthening presence of Christ, the Anointed One.

The reconciliation chapel, a small space designed for the celebration of the sacrament of Reconciliation (confession), is located in the baptismal area whenever possible. This reflects the historical connection between the sacraments of Baptism and Reconciliation.

Point out the altar, the presider's chair, and the lectern or ambo.

Another important area of a Catholic church is the place set aside for the tabernacle. Sometimes this is a side chapel; sometimes it is a prominent place in the sanctuary. The *tabernacle* is the place in which the Eucharist is kept, or reserved. The word comes from the Latin for "tent" or "little house."

Christ becomes present at the Eucharist in several ways. At different times during the eucharistic celebration, our attention is directed to these different ways in which Christ is really present: He is present in the gathered assembly and in the person of the priest. He is present in the Scriptures. He is present most especially under the forms of bread and wine. And as we are commissioned to go out into the world, we find Christ present there also.

Christ is also present in the *Blessed Sacrament*, that is, in the Eucharist reserved in the tabernacle. The Blessed Sacrament is reserved in this way so that the eucharistic Bread may be taken to those who are sick and to those who are dying. In addition the tabernacle has become the focus for the adoration of Christ under the eucharistic species. Catholics have a long tradition of praying before the tabernacle.

A lamp or candle burning before the tabernacle indicates to Catholics that the consecrated Bread is present there. Candles will also be found in other devotional areas and in the assembly area of the Church. At every Mass candles are lit. Once they were used primarily to give light for reading the Scriptures and celebrating the sacred action. Candles have lost much of their practical function, yet their symbolic purpose remains: The beautiful quality of candlelight reminds us of Christ, the Light of the World. As a candle consumes itself in the service of the liturgy, so must we spend ourselves in the service of God and of others.

 Find time this week to make a visit to the Blessed Sacrament. In your prayer tell Jesus anything that is on your mind or in your heart.

Seeing, Hearing, Doing

Like our homes, church buildings can tell us so much just by the way they look. In some older churches, for example, you may find many paintings, statues, mosaics, and perhaps even several altars. Modern churches do not have these. Why are there such differences?

In the early days of the liturgy, when Latin was the spoken language of the congregation, both the ear and the eye had something to do. The ear listened to the meaning of the words, and the eye followed the sacred action. As Latin became less and less understood by the people in the congregation, their ears had less to do. So churches began to be more elaborately decorated to become feasts for the eyes.

In the early Middle Ages, a greater stress began to be placed on the sacrificial dimension of the Eucharist, and Holy Communion was received only by the clergy. Therefore the altar was moved farther away from the faithful and was placed against the wall.

From early times this wall had been decorated with a painting of the cross, the Lamb of God, or Christ in glory. These paintings now began to be placed on the altar itself.

The vestments worn by the priest at the liturgy have their roots in the earliest years of the Church. Originally they came from the way that ordinary people dressed. Today their function has changed. As powerful visible parts of our liturgy, they help us to celebrate the sacred mysteries of the Church. Like everything connected with the liturgy, vestments should be beautiful and well made because they are part of our worship of God.

The altar was filled with statues or paintings: first the crucifixion, then the patron saint of the parish or town. Later other saints were added.

After the Second Vatican Council (1962–65), the bishops determined that the liturgy would once again be celebrated in our own languages. Once again we can understand Sacred Scripture and the prayers at Mass. As our ears became active again, we discovered that sometimes too many decorations in the church could distract us from concentrating on what we were hearing! Today we Catholics are looking for a balance of seeing, hearing, and doing.

Does this mean that newer churches are better than the older ones? Does this mean that churches should have no decoration at all? No, absolutely not. We will not strengthen the ear by starving the eye. No one wants to remove statues and decorations from our churches simply to get rid of them. Statues and beautiful objects of art, banners, and flowers will always be an important part of the environment for our worship.

Many churches have stained-glass windows. In former times the pictures formed by the stained glass, in addition to bathing the assembly area with beautiful light, illustrated Bible stories for those who could not read. But stained-glass windows are not merely history lessons. Their artistic beauty reveals to us something of the beauty of God.

Around the walls of many churches, you will find the stations of the cross. This is a set of pictures, statues, or even simple crosses (numbered from one to fourteen) which mark incidents in the last journey of Jesus to the cross.

This form of devotional prayer became popular in the late Middle Ages. The desire of Christians to follow in the footsteps of Jesus on his way to the cross had led to a long tradition of pilgrimage to the Holy Land. Those who could not afford the expense of the long and dangerous trip to Jerusalem could, by praying the way of the cross, participate in the passion of Jesus in their own villages. Catholics still pray the stations of the cross today, especially during Lent. We go to each station and meditate on an event of the passion. However, the church is primarily a place for our liturgical worship. Personal devotions, such as the stations of the cross, should not distract from the principal purpose of the assembly area.

There is a great variety in the way Catholic churches are decorated. Some are simple, others more elaborate. When we visit the home of friends, we know that the warmth, hospitality, and friendship we experience there are more important than the cost or style of the furniture. In the same way, in a Catholic church the principal beauty is found in the hospitality of our assembly, our devotion to the Eucharist, and the love we carry forth to our brothers and sisters.

Describe those things in your parish church that help you to pray.

Things to SHARE

A church building is both God's house and a house for the Church, the people of God. Some Catholics expect God's house to be a place of silence. Other Catholics expect this gathering space, their house, to be a place where they can greet friends and encourage one another in the Lord. Can both these expectations be met in a way that is both reverent and prayerful?

OnLine WITH THE PARISH

How does your parish church building serve the functions of gathering, storytelling, meal sharing, and commissioning? Do the areas for Baptism, Reconciliation, and reservation of the Eucharist match those described in this chapter?

YOU ARE MY WITNESSES

Scripture & My Life

An image from the Bible that tells us about our union with Christ is that of a "building." Saint Peter told the first Christians, "Like living stones, let yourselves be built into a spiritual house to be a holy priesthood to offer spiritual sacrifices" (1 Peter 2:5). And in the preface for the Dedication of a Church we pray,

You continue to build your
   Church with chosen stones,
   enlivened by the Spirit,
   and cemented together by love.

What does it mean to you to be a "living stone"?

Catholic Teachings

About Churches

The Eucharist not only remembers and makes present the past (the Last Supper) but it also makes present the future, our banquet with Christ in heaven. The church building that houses the Blessed Sacrament is a sign of this future banquet, the world to come. When we enter a church, we know that we are entering a very special, "heavenly" place, a symbol of the Father's house toward which we are journeying.

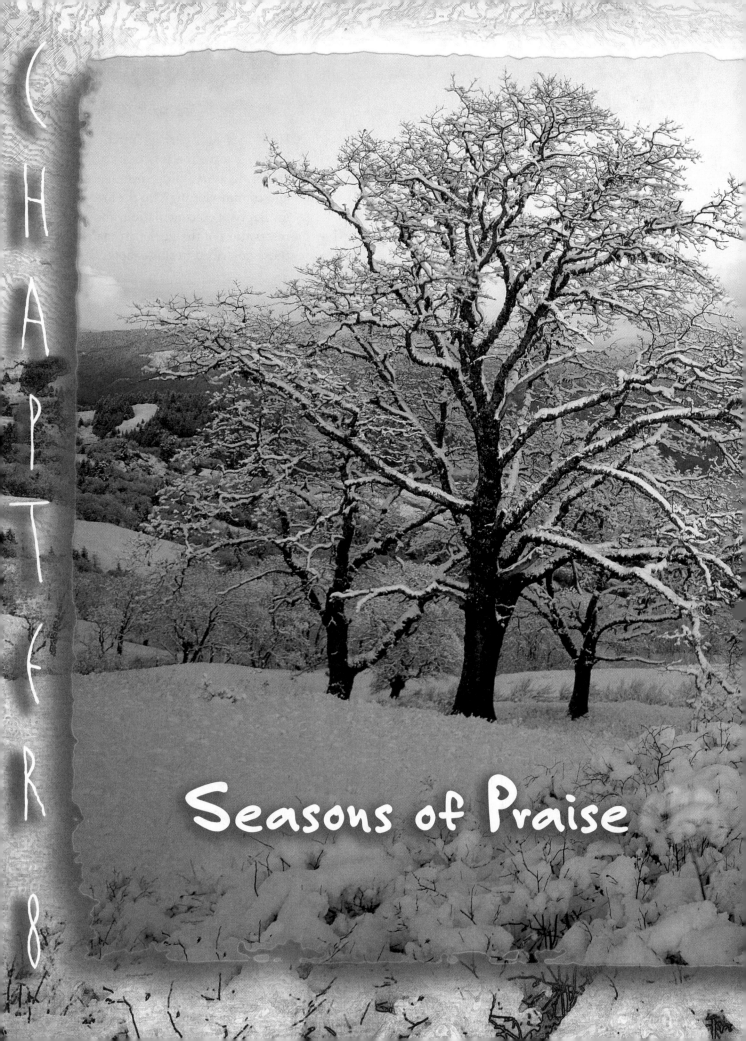

CHAPTER 8

Seasons of Praise

Every day I will bless you;
I will praise your name forever.

Psalm 145:2

The seasons of the year move in a natural cycle—coming to life, growing, flowering, dying, being born again. Do you see this same cycle in your own life?

The Liturgical Seasons

Our life of prayer in the Church follows the same beautiful cycle of coming to life, growing, flowering, dying, being born again. Just as the seasons give variety to nature, the seasons of the liturgical year (the Church's year) give variety to the liturgy. Our life of prayer has its seasons also.

The two principal seasons of the liturgical year are formed around the two great feasts of Easter and Christmas. First we will explore the season of Easter and its preparation period, Lent. Then we will look at the season of Christmas and its preparation time, Advent. Finally we will explore Ordinary Time, the period between the Lent-Easter season and the Advent-Christmas season.

We can see a certain parallel with the birth, life, death cycle of the natural year. We can think of two great moments, birth and death, separated by the ongoing experiences of growing and changing. The Church year, then, has two main seasons, Lent-Easter and Advent-Christmas, separated by two seasons of Ordinary Time.

The seasons of the Church year do not exist simply for the sake of variety or change; they serve a much deeper purpose. As we have learned, each time we celebrate the liturgy, we celebrate the paschal mystery of Christ. In the liturgical year, the Church unfolds the entire mystery of Christ. This mystery is so complex and rich in meaning that no one single prayer or liturgical celebration can ever express it adequately.

The liturgical year helps us to "walk around" the paschal mystery. During the course of a year, we view it from different angles, in different lights. Within the cycle of a year, the Church unfolds the whole mystery of Christ, from his incarnation and birth until his ascension, the day of Pentecost, and the expectation of his return in glory.

The liturgy enables us to pass from our past-present-future concept of time into God's time of salvation, so that the grace and mystery of the event remembered are in some way made present. When we hear the passion of Christ proclaimed on Good Friday and sing "Were You There When They Crucified My Lord?" the answer is *yes*! You were there! You are there now! You do not have to feel disappointed that all the wonderful events of our faith happened long before you were born. These wonderful events of Christianity are happening now, *today*.

Before we look at the various seasons of the liturgical year, we will look at the word that gives us the key to understanding why we have a liturgical year in the first place. That word is *today*. A prayer from the psalm that we often find in the liturgy is:

> Oh, that today you would hear his voice:
> Do not harden your hearts. . . .
> Psalm 95:7–8

The liturgical year, with its various feasts and seasons, helps us to keep our hearts open *each day* to the voice of God in our lives and in our world.

The Lord's Day

When most Catholics think of the major feasts of the liturgical year, they usually think of Christmas and Easter. But the *original* Christian feast day is Sunday. Sunday is the key to the whole liturgical year.

At the time of Jesus, Sunday was called "the first day of the week." The other days were simply numbered in order: the second day, the third day, and so on. The only day given a special name was the seventh day, the Sabbath. Each of the four

gospels mentions explicitly that the resurrection of Jesus took place on "the first day of the week"— that is, Sunday.

The Christian celebration of Sunday has a different focus from the Jewish sabbath. Jews rest on the sabbath because God rested on the seventh day: "God blessed the seventh day and made it holy, because on it he rested from all the work he had done in creation" (Genesis 2:3). The Christian Sunday is primarily a day to assemble for worship. At first the Christian Sunday was a workday like the other days of the week; only later did it take on the Jewish characteristic of a day of rest.

The Sunday assembly for Eucharist is at the very heart of the meaning of Sunday. As we sit at the eucharistic table—with Jesus, with the disciples, with all those who believed in the resurrection throughout ages past, and with all those who will believe in ages to come—past, present, and future become one. We come to the table of the One who died in the past and taste the future banquet of heaven. We sing of our confidence in life:

Dying you destroyed our death,
rising you restored our life.

We sing of our freedom:

Lord, by your cross and resurrection
you have set us free.

In which eucharistic acclamation do we proclaim our faith that Christ will come again?

Day of Resurrection

What we think about Sunday depends on what we think about the resurrection. Do you believe in the resurrection? If you are a Christian, you will surely answer yes to that question. But what if we ask, "Do you believe in the resurrection not only as a historical event but also as happening *now*?"

What does it mean to believe that the resurrection is now? Consider this: Have you ever watched a movie that you have seen before? In spite of all the twists and turns of plot, you already know that everything turns out all right in the end. In the same way, the resurrection tells us that everything will turn out more than "all right" for us. The resurrection tells us that sorrow will be overwhelmed by joy, loss by victory, and death by new life. This is the role the resurrection of Jesus plays in our daily lives.

CHRIST HAS DIED   CHRIST IS RISEN   CHRIST WILL COME AGAIN

There are times when life can be discouraging and the world disappointing. There are times when we look around us and see so much pain and violence that we are tempted to wonder: Is death winning the battle? But in the midst of all that is evil in the world, the resurrection is God's great cry of triumph. The resurrection is our proof that life has a happy ending. The risen Jesus is our proof that loving and forgiving one another even as God loves and forgives us is a road that leads, not to death, but to life. The resurrection lets us know that God is in charge. Sin and evil will never win in the end. God's love and life will triumph.

The Lenten Retreat

Lent is the time of preparation for the celebration of Easter. It begins on Ash Wednesday and extends to Holy Thursday. Lent is like a retreat. It is a time of prayer, fasting, and almsgiving (which means sharing what we have with the poor).

66

When you hear the word *Lent*, what picture comes to mind? Penance, purple, fish, ashes, fasting, sacrifice, giving up movies? These are the images many Catholics associate with Lent. But your idea of Lent will be closer to the Church's meaning of the season if the first thing that comes to your mind is an image of new life—of Baptism. Baptism provides the key to Lent.

We have seen that in the fourth and fifth centuries, the Church developed liturgies to assist people who wanted to become Christians. The final forty days of this faith journey, the final "forty-day retreat" before Baptism, became what we now call Lent. Lent is the time for the catechumens to continue their preparation for Baptism, Confirmation, and Eucharist. It is a time for those of us who are already baptized to reaffirm what this sacrament means in our lives today.

For some Christians, Baptism is an event that happened long ago and does not have much impact on what they do today. But Baptism, as we have seen, changes us so radically that we are different, "marked" forever. Baptism gives us the spiritual mark that we call *character*. We are "characterized" by the life of Jesus that we find in the gospels. Once we are baptized, the promises of our Baptism should influence our decisions for the rest of our lives.

When we understand Baptism as the focus of Lent, the things we choose to give up can be more clearly understood. Our Lenten sacrifices are not a negative giving up of something. Rather, they direct us to a positive goal, joyful union with God.

Dying and Rising
Baptism is both a dying and a rising. Saint Paul says, "If, then, we have died with Christ, we believe that we shall also live with him" (Romans 6:8). The penitential aspect of Lent, the "giving something up" part, is related to the dying aspect of Baptism. But the "dying" is not an end in itself. We need to keep our eyes fixed on the "rising" that Baptism offers us.

But death, in whatever form it comes, is never easy. Sometimes we resist change in our lives, even change for the better. Jesus promises us that life will spring out of death: "Unless a grain of wheat falls to the ground and dies, it remains just a grain of wheat; but if it dies, it produces much fruit" (John 12:24). The intention of the farmer is not to kill the seed. Yet in order to grow, the seed must change its life-form. It cannot remain the same old seed!

Here is another example. When you were in the first grade, you were at the bottom of the heap; everybody else was older and seemed stronger and smarter. But now, just when it seems that you are at the top, you have to start over again in high school.

What if you would decide that you want to stay where you are, where you are comfortable? You would probably be told, "Give it up! Move on!"

Sometimes we get attached to something that keeps us from moving on. We can get caught at a particular stage of growth in our Christian lives. But during Lent we may hear the voice of the Spirit tell us, "Give it up! Move on!"

For most of us, moving on involves letting go of something *good* in order to get *an even greater good*. It means planting small seeds and looking forward to a good harvest.

 Is there something now that keeps you from moving on in your faith? Write about it in your journal.

The laws of fast and abstinence call us to reflection, sorrow for sin, and a more serious approach to Christian life.

In the United States, Catholics who have completed their fourteenth year are bound by the law of abstinence on Ash Wednesday and all Fridays during Lent. Abstinence means that on these days we do not eat meat. Ash Wednesday and Good Friday are also days on which Catholics over eighteen are bound to fast (that is, to eat only one full meal).

The Triduum

Did you know that the oldest Christian feast is Sunday? Jesus rose on the Sunday after the Passover, and, remembering this, Christians began to celebrate the Sunday closest to the Jewish Passover with special solemnity. This "Christian Passover" became what we now call Easter.

The Christian Passover soon became the special time to celebrate the sacrament of Baptism, the sacrament of our passing over from death to life in Christ. As the rites and celebrations surrounding Christian initiation grew and developed, the Christian community found that one twenty-four-hour day was simply not enough time to experience the mystery, and the celebration was extended to three days. Today we call this celebration the *Triduum*, from the Latin word meaning "three days."

The three-day observance begins with the Mass of the Lord's Supper in the evening on Holy Thursday and ends with evening prayer on Easter Sunday. The solemn liturgies of the Triduum are the most important liturgies of the Church year. The washing of the feet after the gospel of Holy Thursday is followed by the reading of the Passion and the adoration of the cross on Good Friday. At the Easter Vigil, the darkness and grief of Good Friday is broken by the blessing of the new fire and the paschal candle, the singing of the Easter Proclamation, the first sounds of the "Alleluia," and the sacramental initiation of the catechumens.

These are ceremonies we can experience at no other time during the year. They teach us the meaning of Christ's life, death, and resurrection, not in words alone, but in symbols and rituals: in fire, in water, in darkness, in light, in walking, in kneeling, in standing again.

It takes a special kind of attention and alertness to enter into these mysteries. How can we come to these events fully aware and prepared? The Church recommends that we fast, especially on Good Friday and, where possible, Holy Saturday as well. This fasting is very different from dieting. The purpose of fasting is not to lose weight; its purpose is to gain insight into the mysteries of the Triduum. It is a fast of awareness. It creates a hunger that can be satisfied only by the best of foods: our Easter Eucharist, which we share with those who join us at our eucharistic table for the very first time.

Catholics eighteen years of age and under are not obliged to fast, but even younger Catholics can prepare, through prayer and simple acts of love and selflessness, to celebrate the Triduum with an open heart and a clear mind.

As a group, plan ways you will prepare during Lent this year to celebrate the Triduum together in your parish.

Things to SHARE

What do you and your family do to make Sunday different from the other days of the week? In what practical ways do you abstain from work and other concerns that would keep you from praying and relaxing on the Lord's Day?

What happens if work is necessary on Sunday? If this is the case in your family, how do you celebrate Sunday? How does your family pray and relax?

OnLine WITH THE PARISH

The liturgical year is a construct; it has to be "made." Often, at the change of the liturgical seasons, there is a lot of work to be done in your parish church in order to enable the liturgical season to come alive for the parishioners. These are especially good times to volunteer your services to help clean and decorate the church for Lent, the Triduum, Advent, or Christmas.

YOU ARE MY WITNESSES

Scripture of My Life

A scriptural theme of the Triduum is the symbol of the Lamb of God. On Holy Thursday the reading recalls the Passover lamb (Exodus 12:1–8); on Good Friday "the suffering servant" is compared to a lamb (Isaiah 53:7). At the Easter Vigil the proclamation reminds us:

This is our passover feast,
   when Christ, the true Lamb,
      is slain. . . .

On Easter Sunday we sing the praises of Jesus Christ, the victorious Lamb.

Catholic Teachings

About Sunday

The most important way Catholics praise God and honor the risen Christ is by participating in the Eucharist, our source of strength and joy. This is the obligation of every Catholic. This means that, except for a serious reason, we must worship God at the liturgy. Our Sunday celebration can be enriched by spending time with our families and by setting aside extra quiet time for prayer and reading.

A Year of Glory

Praise the LORD, all you nations!
Give glory, all you peoples!
The LORD'S love for us is strong;
the LORD is faithful forever.
Hallelujah!

Psalm 117

"There is a season, turn, turn, turn . . .
And a time for every purpose under heaven."©

(Song lyrics adapted from Ecclesiastes 3:1)

How do these words suggest
that we live in a world of time,
of change, of new beginnings?

The Great Fifty Days

We human beings don't usually like sudden
changes. We like predictable changes. We like to
know ahead of time that a change is coming so that
we can prepare for it. The seasons of the Church
year are seasons of change, seasons of preparation,
and seasons of new beginnings.

At the heart of our Christian life is the belief that
God has radically changed the universe through
the paschal mystery of Jesus. We call this radical
change *salvation*. It is the focus of our Easter
celebration.

Easter is "the Feast of feasts,' the 'Solemnity of solemnities'" (*Catechism*, 1169). Easter is so important that we cannot even begin to celebrate it adequately in one day. It takes a "week of weeks." It takes fifty days, a *Pentecost* (from the Greek word meaning "fifty"). *Each day* of these fifty days is Easter.

At the Easter Vigil we received new members into our community through the sacraments of initiation. During their time of preparation, the catechumens learned about the sacraments "from outside," as it were. Now, as *neophytes* (newly initiated Christians), they experience the sacraments of Baptism and Eucharist "from within" the community.

For the neophytes (and for us as well) this fifty-day season of Easter is the time of mystagogy. *Mystagogy* is a time for learning about and reflecting on the mysteries of faith. The Easter season is a time for the community and the neophytes to grow in their understanding of the paschal mystery. It is a time to make the paschal mystery part of our lives through meditation on the gospel, sharing in the Eucharist, and doing good works.

The newly baptized have not only "put on Christ"; they have also put on his body, the Church. They have joined a new family. And they (and we) take time during these fifty days to learn who that family, that Church, is. We find the picture of the birth and early growth of the Church in the Acts of the Apostles.

The Story Continues

The Acts of the Apostles forms one story with the Gospel of Luke. If you compare the way the two parts of this story (Luke 1:1–4 and Acts 1:1–2) begin, it is clear that Luke/Acts is meant to be read as a unit. Luke/Acts is a very special form of writing. The author wants to show three things: (1) the life and deeds of Jesus, (2) how his life and deeds were continued in the lives and deeds of the first disciples, and (3) how his life and deeds are to be continued by us in the Church today.

In Luke's Gospel we see Jesus healing the sick; in Acts we see Peter doing the same. In the gospel we see Jesus brought before the high priest to be interrogated; in Acts we see the same thing happening to Peter. The death of Stephen, the first martyr, parallels the death of Jesus. Stephen prays, "Lord, do not hold this sin against them" (Acts 7:60) as Jesus had prayed "Father, forgive them, they know not what they do" (Luke 23:34).

Why did Luke write in this way? He wanted to show us that what Jesus did during his lifetime, the first disciples also did during theirs, and we—today's disciples—are to do during ours! As we hear readings from the Acts of the Apostles proclaimed at each Mass during the great fifty days, we might ask ourselves these questions: "Is this our Church family today?" "Are we a healing Church?" "Are we a forgiving Church?" The stories in Acts are not simply stories of long-ago people and places. They are *our* stories, *our* pictures. The challenge of the great fifty days of Easter is to continue the story of Luke/Acts today, in our Church and in our lives.

Filled with the Spirit

On the final day of our fifty-day celebration of Easter, we celebrate Pentecost. As with each feast and each liturgical season of the year, its meaning is best understood by looking at the Scripture readings. The readings for Pentecost speak of the sending of the Holy Spirit. The word *spirit* is a translation of the Hebrew word *ruah*, which means "breath," "air," or "wind."

In the second reading for Pentecost, we read about the descent of the Holy Spirit upon the disciples: As they were gathered together, they heard a noise like a strong wind (*ruah*). "Then there appeared to them tongues as of fire. . . . And they were all filled with the holy Spirit and began to speak in different tongues, as the Spirit enabled them to proclaim" (Acts 2:3–4). Right away we begin to see the gifts and graces of the Spirit at work in the Church.

In the gospel for Pentecost, we read John's account of Jesus giving the Holy Spirit. On the evening of the first day of the week, "Jesus came and stood in their midst and said to them, 'Peace be with you. . . . As the Father has sent me, so I send you.' And . . . he breathed [*ruah*] on them and said to them, 'Receive the holy Spirit'" (John 20:19–22). Sins are to be forgiven! The gifts of peace and reconciliation are given to the Church.

The liturgy combines these accounts in order that we might reflect and ask ourselves: "How does the Holy Spirit act in the Church today?" "How does the Spirit come to me?" The liturgy makes Pentecost present to us now, today.

Our understanding of the work of the Holy Spirit today comes from three sources. The first is the witness of the Scriptures, which we have briefly explored. The second is the public prayer of the Church, the liturgy. The third is our own lives and experience.

Let us consider the prayer of the Church. In Eucharistic Prayer IV we speak directly to God and recall Jesus' sending us the Holy Spirit:

> And that we might live no longer for
>   ourselves but for him,
> he sent the Holy Spirit from you, Father,
> as his first gift to those who believe,
> to complete his work on earth
> and bring us the fullness of grace.

What can we learn from this prayer? First we learn that the Holy Spirit is not the possession of an exceptional few. The Holy Spirit is given to *every* Christian, to all who believe.

The gift of the Holy Spirit is a gift of *mission*. When Jesus gave the Holy Spirit, he told the disciples, "As the Father has sent me, so I send you" (John 20:21). What the Father gave Jesus to do, the risen Lord commissions us to continue. This is the message of Pentecost. This is the work of the Holy Spirit. This is the work of a lifetime.

 The Holy Spirit works with each one of us for the good of all. How is the Spirit breathing life into you?

Madonna of the Chair, Raphael, circa 1514

Advent and Christmas

During Advent we go back to the beginning. We do not forget that we are celebrating the same Jesus who died and rose for us but we remember also that he chose to share ordinary human life with us. He chose to become one of us and to experience life as we do: its joys, sorrows, disappointments, hopes.

Advent is a time of joyful expectation. What do we expect, and why are we joyful? The answer to these questions is given in the Scriptures proposed for the season.

From the First Sunday of Advent until December 16, the readings express the hope and longing for that day when the plan of God will be completed. We dream of how things ought to be and long for the day when Christ will come again in glory. From December 17 to December 24, the readings direct our attention to the birth of Jesus.

The prophet Isaiah sets the tone for Advent. He voices the hope and longing of God's people, wandering far away from home, in exile in a foreign land. They want to return home. They dream of the day when God's rule will prevail and wars will end. God's people long for the time when all hatred and prejudice will cease, when the streets will be safe and children will not live in fear.

How and when will this all come about? We do not know. Asked by the Pharisees when God's reign would come, Jesus replied, "Behold, the kingdom of God is among you" (Luke 17:21).

How can the kingdom be among us when the world is so full of sin and violence? To see the kingdom, we need a special kind of light: faith. The light of Advent (as symbolized in the Advent wreath and in all the other beautiful lights we see at this time of year) little by little replaces the darkness of doubt and discouragement. By the light of faith, we see the kingdom.

Christmas, then, is a celebration of light— the light of Christ, the Word made flesh. In the birth of Jesus, the invisible God becomes visible. In the life of Jesus, we see God's plan for the world unfold. This plan is revealed gently and quietly, even as God gently and quietly appeared among us in the stable at Bethlehem.

In our lives, too, God's plan is usually revealed gently and quietly: in a quiet moment of prayer, in the stillness after the loss of a friend, in those minutes at night before we fall asleep. Little by little we are to grow into the likeness of Christ.

Christmas is the season when we pray fervently for the final revelation of God's mysterious plan. We pray for an end to war, hunger, and injustice. We pray, *Marana tha!* "Come, Lord Jesus!"

CATHOLIC ID

White, red, green, violet—what do these liturgical colors mean? Red (the color of fire) symbolizes the Holy Spirit, and is used on Pentecost and for the sacrament of Confirmation. Red (the color of blood) is also used on days when we celebrate the passion of Jesus (for example, on Passion Sunday and Good Friday) and on days when we celebrate the feasts of martyrs. White, the color of joy and victory, is used for the other feasts of the Lord, Mary, and the other saints. White is also used for the seasons of Easter and Christmas. Violet is used for the seasons of Lent and Advent. Green, the color of life and hope, is used during Ordinary Time.

Have you ever noticed how often at Mass we pray for the coming of Christ? Can you recall a few examples?

Ordinary Time

What is Ordinary Time? If we take *ordinary* to mean "usual, average, of inferior quality or second-rate," it will be hard to get excited about Ordinary Time. However, these days are not ordinary in that sense. *Ordinary* here means "not seasonal." *Ordinary Time* is the time that lies outside the seasons of Lent-Easter and Advent-Christmas. In Ordinary Time, the Church celebrates the mystery of Christ not in one specific aspect but in all its aspects.

During the *seasons* of the Church year, the readings from Scripture are chosen according to the theme of the season: Lent, Baptism; Easter, resurrection; the great fifty days of Easter, Acts of the Apostles; Advent, Isaiah and joyful expectation; Christmas, God's taking flesh. During Ordinary Time the readings are not chosen according to a theme. Rather, in Ordinary Time we read from the various books of the Bible from beginning to end in a continuous fashion. This is the key to understanding Ordinary Time.

In Ordinary Time we concentrate for an entire year on the life and work of Jesus Christ as proclaimed in one of the Gospels, either Matthew,

Mark, or Luke. (John's Gospel is read principally during the liturgical seasons.) As we meet Christ in the Scriptures, we come to know him better. Knowledge of the Scriptures is knowledge of Christ.

Ordinary Time enables us to hear the whole gospel—not just the "big stories" of birth, death, and resurrection, but all the "in between" stories, parables, and teachings. Our Christian life is not just Christmas and Easter. It is all the days in between, the ordinary days. And perhaps that is what makes it difficult.

The hardest part of following Jesus is simply that, for the most part, it is so terribly ordinary! Getting up every morning and going to school, treating others with respect and fairness, doing homework and chores every night, practicing a musical instrument day after day, showing up for sports practice night after night—these things seem so ordinary, so routine, and possibly even boring. However, we know that the truly valuable things in our lives are achieved just that way: little by little, day after day.

For the most part God is not revealed in the spectacular or the sensational. Rather, the miracle of the kingdom is found in our daily efforts and everyday growth. We take up our cross daily and allow God's Spirit to help us grow gradually into the likeness of Jesus.

Read Mark 4:4–20, the parable of the sower. Think of God's word "sown" in your heart. What kind of soil has it fallen on?

The seasons of life happen "naturally," but the seasons of the Church year need our help. How can you "help Advent happen" in your home? A symbol that many families use is the Advent wreath. The circle, the evergreen branches, the increasing light each week—each of these symbols reflects the themes of Advent. Do you keep this custom in your home?

OnLine WITH THE PARISH

How can you help your parish celebrate Advent and Christmas? By cleaning and decorating the church? By joining the youth choir? By helping with a parish action for the poor? Lend your time and talents!

YOU ARE MY WITNESSES

Scripture & My Life

The Holy Spirit equips us for our mission by giving us seven gifts, or *charisms*. The gifts of the Holy Spirit are wisdom, understanding, right judgment, courage, knowledge, reverence, and wonder and awe in the presence of the Lord. The source of these traditional names is Isaiah 11:2–3.

The gifts of the Spirit do not work automatically, of course. It is up to us to develop these gifts and to use them for our own spiritual growth and for the service of God and others.

Catholic Teachings

About Angels

What does the Church believe about angels? We believe that angels are spirits created by God to be his servants and messengers. Angels assure us that God is concerned about us. Even their names speak of God: *Gabriel* means "strength of God," *Raphael* means "God's healing," and *Michael* means, "Who is like God?"

The whole Church benefits from the help of the angels, and each of us here on earth has an angel "as protector and shepherd" to guide us on the path of life (*Catechism*, 334, 336).

The Sacrament of Reconciliation

Lord, you are kind and forgiving,
most loving to all who call on you.

Psalm 86:5

Some people were shocked when they learned
that Pope John Paul II had gone to the jail cell of the
man who tried to assassinate him. They were even more
shocked when they found out that the pope forgave
the man. Why do you think the pope did this?
Are forgiveness and mercy so important in our lives?

Christ and the Samaritan Woman at the Well, Paolo Veronese, sixteenth century

Rich in Mercy

When the writers of Sacred Scripture wanted to describe their experience of God's love and mercy, they used some very dramatic imagery. When God forgives and removes our sins, he is described as putting them "as far as the east is from the west" (Psalm 103:12). Our God is truly a God of compassion!

Jesus wanted us to experience this forgiveness of God even more in our lives. Only God can forgive sins, and this is why Jesus, God's only Son, came among us. He wanted to free us from sin, to heal our wounded and broken natures. Who else but Jesus told the stories of the lost sheep and the

prodigal son (Luke 15:1–7, 11–32)? He wanted us to know how much God loves us.

After Christ's resurrection the early Church community recognized what he had done for them. By offering his life for us on the cross, Jesus had redeemed us. He had reconciled us to God and to one another. This means that in Christ we were brought back again into friendship with God. We first share in this reconciliation and forgiveness at Baptism. But what about the sins we commit after Baptism?

We need to be healed over and over again. We need to turn to Jesus, who is the sacrament of God's

forgiveness. How do we do this? Jesus entrusted his Church with the mission of healing and forgiveness, especially in the sacraments. In the Eucharist we share in Christ's Body and Blood, given for us and shed for the forgiveness of sins. In the Eucharist we realize and share in the peace Christ gave to us.

Jesus did not stop there, however. He gave his apostles and their successors the power to forgive sins. On Easter night Jesus appeared to his apostles and breathed on them. He said, "Receive the holy Spirit. Whose sins you forgive are forgiven them, and whose sins you retain are retained" (John 20:22–23). This same Holy Spirit makes our hearts ready to receive God's forgiveness. And we do this in a most wonderful way in a special sacrament.

Actually we may know this sacrament by many names. It is called the *sacrament of Reconciliation* because through it our relationship to God and to the community of the Church is restored. This sacrament is also called the sacrament of *Penance*. Penance celebrates our continuing conversion, our turning from selfishness and sin to the spirit of love and generosity. The word *penance* can also mean that part of the sacrament in which the priest asks us to say certain prayers or to perform some other action to help atone for our sins.

For many years most Catholics called the sacrament *Confession. Confession*, however, names only one part of the sacrament and not the most important part at that. *Reconciliation* names what is most important, what Jesus does. Sinners are brought back to God and to the community. They are reconciled.

The sacrament of Reconciliation is a beautiful celebration of love and forgiveness. The sacrament is never meant to make us feel false guilt or to become overly concerned with sin. Nor is the sacrament meant to make us blame ourselves for things beyond our control. The Church teaches us that it is meant for healing what is broken, for setting free that which

is bound up. In addition this sacrament is not just intended for the times when we commit serious, or mortal, sin. Whenever we confess our venial sins, we are strengthened and grow in God's grace.

Let's look more closely at the celebration of Reconciliation in the life of the Church.

A Reconciling Church

Over the centuries the way the sacrament of Reconciliation was celebrated changed and developed. The basic elements of the sacrament, however, remain. There must be a conversion, a turning, to God; a confession of sins to a priest; a penance to show sorrow for sin and a decision to avoid sin; a reconciliation to God and to anyone harmed by sin; and forgiveness of sin.

In our parishes today we go to confession face-to-face with a priest or from behind a screen. Often communal penance celebrations are held, always accompanied by individual confessions to a priest. The sacrament of Reconciliation is a sacrament of healing, a sacrament of joy and peace. In it our sins are forgiven and we are restored to friendship with God, with others, and with ourselves.

The Communal Rite

The Second Vatican Council revised the rites for Reconciliation to express more clearly what the sacrament really means and what it really does. These rites show that the sacrament is clearly a liturgical act. Like the Eucharist, Reconciliation celebrates the paschal mystery of Christ. Like the Eucharist, it consists of four parts: gathering, storytelling, the sacramental action, and commissioning.

There is no "one way" to celebrate this sacrament. Here is a general description of the *communal* celebration of the sacrament of Reconciliation.

Gathering   The community gathers at the appointed time. There is a minister of hospitality at the door of the church to welcome us and to distribute any materials we may need to participate in the sacrament. The introductory rites usually include a hymn, a liturgical greeting, and a prayer by the priest to gather the assembly together.

Storytelling   Once we are gathered, we tell the stories of God's love and mercy that are recorded in the Bible. In hearing these stories of God's love, we come to see how much we are loved and to realize how little we have loved in return. The difference between these two loves—*how much* God has loved us and *how little* we have loved him—is called the "sense of sin." This is an important part of the

sacramental process. It is the word of God that helps us to know our sinfulness.

Sin must be understood in relation to love. God has loved us so much, and we have so often failed to return that love. When we examine our lives in the light of the message of Jesus, we find that Jesus calls us to wholeness, to maturity. He came that we might have life and have it abundantly. For the Christian sin is not merely breaking the rules; it is the failure to grow. Sin is being today just as you were yesterday. Sin is the failure to respond to the love God has shown us in Christ Jesus.

After we have heard how much God loves us, we examine our lives to see how well we have loved God and our brothers and sisters in return. We examine our conscience in the light of the Scriptures. Together we express our sorrow in an Act of Contrition. Then we each confess our sins to a priest in private and hear the proclamation of God's forgiveness (absolution): "I *absolve* you."

 In what ways do the Scriptures help us prepare for Reconciliation?

The Sacramental Action   This prayer of absolution is the central prayer and sign of the sacrament of Reconciliation.

As in all liturgical prayers, the prayer of absolution is directed to the Blessed Trinity. It also mentions the principal effects of the sacrament: forgiveness, pardon, and peace.

The prayer of absolution that we hear each time we celebrate the sacrament is this:

God, the Father of mercies,
through the death and resurrection of his Son
has reconciled the world to himself
and sent the Holy Spirit among us
for the forgiveness of sins;
through the ministry of the Church
may God give you pardon and peace,
and I absolve you from your sins
in the name of the Father, and of the Son,†
and of the Holy Spirit.

Our response is "Amen."

We have responded to the word of God by confessing our sins and receiving God's forgiveness. Now we celebrate this forgiveness, for it is God's response to *our* word. This part of the celebration might include a hymn, a proclamation of praise and thanksgiving for God's mercy, the Lord's Prayer, the kiss of peace, a song of thanksgiving, and a concluding prayer.

Commissioning The communal rite of Reconciliation concludes with prayers, blessings, and dismissal.

Conversion of Heart

Catholics celebrate Reconciliation even when they have less serious sins to confess. Why? Because this sacrament is a great help to what Jesus wants for all his followers: conversion of heart.

In the life of the Church, the primary moment of conversion is the moment of Baptism. Yet conversion is not limited to that moment. It is the work of a lifetime. As followers of Christ we are called to a continual conversion of heart. One big "turning toward" God at Baptism is not enough for a full Christian life. We must continually turn toward God, as a growing plant continually turns toward its source of light, growth, and energy.

Conversion is a grace of the Holy Spirit. Under the Spirit's guidance we are led to right thinking and good action. And with

The priest is strictly forbidden to use *in any way* anything he hears in the sacrament of Reconciliation. He can never, *never*, NEVER tell anyone what sin you confessed. If he does so, he himself commits a mortal sin. This obligation and promise is called the *seal of confession*. That is, the priest's lips are sealed, and he cannot reveal your sin or your identity.

the help of the Spirit, we find the honesty to admit our failings and the courage to promise to do better. The sacrament of Reconciliation keeps us on track in our own individual work of conversion. It helps us to stop and reflect on how far we have come, and it helps us to resolve to continue the journey.

When the Fathers of the Church explained Baptism, they imagined an individual in the midst of a shipwreck. How to be saved in the midst of a raging sea? Grab a plank! This first plank is the sacrament of Baptism. When they taught about the sacrament of Reconciliation, they called it "the second plank" (*Catechism*, 1446). As Christians we need both to keep us afloat.

The Individual Rite

The individual rite of Reconciliation is another way the Church gives us to celebrate this sacrament. There are two important elements to this rite.

The first element is human action: contrition, confession, and satisfaction (doing one's penance). The second element is God's action: the forgiveness of sins through the Church. Both our human actions and God's action are equally essential.

Contrition *Contrition* is sorrow for having sinned, hatred for the sin committed, and a firm decision not to sin again. Before Reconciliation we should take time to make an examination of conscience and to ask ourselves if we really are sorry for our selfish actions and wrong choices.

Confession Confessing our sins to a priest is an essential part of this sacrament because the priest forgives sin in the name of Jesus Christ and the Church. We are the Church, the body of Christ in the world. Sin affects the whole body of Christ. Just as in physical sickness, when one part is in pain, the whole body suffers. The priest represents Christ, so it is his task and joy to welcome sinners, as Jesus did, and to restore them to their rightful place in the body of Christ.

Sometimes people worry about what the priest thinks of them when they tell him their sins. They imagine that the priest sees them at their worst. Actually the very opposite is true. *Everybody* sins, but only *some* sinners are moved to

do penance. When you tell your sins to the priest and express your desire to repent, the priest sees you at your best. The priest sees you, not in your sinning, but in your repentance.

Satisfaction *Satisfaction* is simply repairing, in some way, the harm our sins have done. Returning or paying for stolen goods, for example, is one obvious way of making satisfaction for the sin of stealing.

This kind of satisfaction is usually included in the *penance* given. A penance can be prayer, an offering, works of mercy, service to a neighbor, voluntary self-denial, sacrifices, and most of all a patient acceptance of the ordinary circumstances of our lives.

Reconciliation Now we turn to God's action in the sacrament of Reconciliation: the forgiveness of sins. Through this forgiveness, as Pope John Paul II explained, we are reconciled with self, God, the entire Church, and "with all creation" (*Catechism*, 1469). Reconciliation is a sacrament of peace and comfort, a sacrament sealed in the conversational tones of a human voice: "I absolve you. . . . Go in the peace of Christ."

The symbol of the sacrament of Reconciliation is the symbol of language. How would you explain this statement?

What is helpful to you about talking to a priest? What would you talk to a priest about? As a teenager do you think you would ask advice in the sacrament of Reconciliation more often than you did in elementary school?

When is the sacrament of Reconciliation celebrated in your parish? When are communal celebrations of the sacrament scheduled? When are opportunities available for celebrating the sacrament individually?

The communal celebration requires preparation and planning on the part of the parish liturgical team and also requires ministers: greeters, readers, musicians, and others. Is it possible for you to volunteer to serve in one of these ministries during the celebration?

YOU ARE MY WITNESSES

Scripture of My Life

The gospels clearly show that forgiveness of sins is central to the message of Jesus. Frequently in the gospels we see Jesus forgiving sins. He taught us to pray "Forgive us our trespasses, as we forgive those who trespass against us." And with his dying breath, he forgave even those who had nailed him to the cross.

Catholic Teachings

About Reconciliation

Although confessing our venial sins and daily faults is encouraged, we are only *obliged* to confess individual sins to a priest when we are aware of having committed a *mortal sin* (a serious offense against God, done knowingly and freely, which cuts us off from the life of God and the Church). Catholics who are in the state of mortal sin and physically able must confess the sin to a priest in the sacrament of Reconciliation before they can receive Holy Communion.

The Anointing of the Sick

Even when I walk through a dark valley,
   I fear no harm for you are at my side. . . .
You anoint my head with oil;
   my cup overflows.

Psalm 23:4–5

Julian of Norwich once wrote:
"All will be well, and all will be well, and every kind of thing will be well." Do we really believe this —even in the midst of pain, suffering, and death? These realities can raise questions in our minds: Why do people get sick? Why do they suffer?

The Mystery of Suffering

People have asked questions like these since the beginning of time!

There is no easy answer to the mystery of suffering. It is one of those big questions whose answer is discovered bit by bit through our lived experience.

It is also a dangerous question because we can easily jump to overly simplified (and consequently, wrong) answers: "He got sick because he was bad." "She is ill because God wants her to suffer." It is very dangerous to think in this way, for such thinking leads to false conclusions about suffering and false conclusions about God.

We know that God created us out of love and that creation is holy and good. Suffering and illness do not exist because God wants them to exist. But if they do not come from him, where do they come from?

Sometimes, but not always, they come from our own ignorance and poor decisions. We have the responsibility to care for our bodies, to be attentive to proper nourishment, exercise, rest, and relaxation. Pain is often a message from the body telling us that something is wrong, that something needs to be corrected or cared for.

Human illness can urge us to learn more about the functions of the body through the study of chemistry, biology, physiology, and other sciences. In so doing, perhaps we can help others someday. Even more important, illness is a call to learn more about our inner selves, about life and its meaning.

88

We know that one of the hardest things about being sick is the sudden end to our ordinary activities at school, with friends, in sports, and so on. Much of the way we think about ourselves is tied up with what we can do. When our health is taken away, we find that we cannot do very much! Then we begin to wonder who we really are.

But faith gives us a new way of seeing illness. In God's eyes we are more than what we do, more than our accomplishments. The world often judges people by how much money they make, by how many things they have. Illness can remind us that God loves us for who we are, not for what we have or what we do.

Jesus and Healing

We know about God's love and concern for the sick because we can see it made visible in Jesus. On almost every page of the gospels, we see Jesus bringing health and wholeness to those who are ill and suffering.

Look, for example, at the first chapter of Mark's Gospel. After Jesus called the first disciples, he cured a man with an unclean spirit; then he cured Peter's mother-in-law, who was in bed with a fever. Mark continues: "When it was evening, after sunset, they brought to him all who were ill or possessed by demons. The whole town was gathered at the door. He cured many who were sick with various diseases, and he drove out many demons" (1:32–34).

Jesus has hardly begun his ministry, but already he is known as someone who heals the sick and cares for them. Jesus himself is a visible sign of God's desire for our health and wholeness. When we see Jesus as a sign of God's healing, we are well on our way to understanding the Church as a sign of healing. The Church exercises this ministry in many ways and celebrates it in the sacrament of the Anointing of the Sick.

Healing in the Early Church

Jesus' desire to heal the sick did not stop when he ascended into heaven. He had told his disciples to continue this work: "So. . . . they anointed with oil many who were sick and cured them" (Mark 6:12–13).

In the Letter of James, we read of the way in which one early Christian community continued this healing work of Jesus. "Is anyone among you sick? He should summon the presbyters of the church, and they should pray over him and anoint [him] with oil in the name of the Lord, and the prayer of faith will save the sick person, and the Lord will raise him up. If he has committed any sins, he will be forgiven" (James 5:14–15).

James tells us that prayer is necessary in every situation in our lives: when we are well, when we are sick, and at every moment in between. It is in this context of prayer that James tells us of his

Jesus Heals a Blind Man,
Duccio di Buoninsegna,
thirteenth century

89

One of the ways in which we Catholics show our concern for the sick is our practice of having priests, deacons, or eucharistic ministers bring Holy Communion to them in their homes or in the hospital. In this way they are united to the Lord in the sacrament of the Eucharist and also to the community of believers. In some parishes the eucharistic ministers come forward before the dismissal and are given the Eucharist to bring to the sick.

What are some other ways in which we show our concern for the sick?

community's practice of praying for the sick. The sick person calls for the priests. When they arrive, they pray. The phrase "pray over" the sick person suggests a laying on of hands, the ancient sign of blessing. They anoint the sick person with oil.

When priests and teachers later explained the meaning of the rites of anointing, they drew a parallel between physical healing by medical doctors and spiritual healing administered by the Church. Many good things can be learned from this analogy. But one bad effect it had was that the Church's anointing was put off as long as possible, just as going to the doctor was put off until the sick person was at death's door. The sacramental anointing (*unction* in Latin) came to be called *Extreme Unction*, the last anointing. The sacrament for the *sick* became a sacrament only for the *dying*. The priest's final absolution of our sins and this anointing at the time of death came to be called the *last rites*.

The focus of the sacrament then changed from physical healing to spiritual healing, to the forgiveness of sins. The public, liturgical rite of the early Church became a private ceremony. Often only the priest and the dying person were present. Extreme Unction had become more private than public, more fearful than joyful, and more dreaded than celebrated. For many Catholics, when the

priest arrived with the holy oil for the last rites, it was a sure sign of death.

However, following the liturgical reforms of the Second Vatican Council, Extreme Unction became once again the sacrament of the Anointing of the Sick as we know it today.

 Take a moment to think of those "among you" who are sick. Pray for them now.

The Second Vatican Council made three important changes in the rite of the sacrament.

First, it was important to teach that this sacrament is not just intended for the dying, that it is primarily a sacrament of healing for all Christians who are seriously ill. It can be received more than once—each time, in fact, that a Christian becomes seriously ill, and again if the illness worsens. So the Council suggested that we call this sacrament not Extreme Unction but the sacrament of the *Anointing of the Sick*.

Second, this sacrament of healing was restored to its liturgical setting. No longer was it to be considered a private action between the priest and the sick person. The community's role of prayerful support was restored, and the celebration of the Anointing of the Sick within the Eucharist was encouraged.

Third, the focus of the sacrament was directed once again toward *healing*. In anointing the hands of the sick, the priest leads the community in prayer. We pray that our sick brothers and sisters will be raised up to share in the life of the resurrected Jesus—both physically and spiritually.

Celebration of Anointing

The celebration of the sacrament may take place at a Sunday or weekday Mass in a parish church, in the home of the sick person, in the hospital, or in an emergency situation. Here is a general description of the way the sacrament is celebrated at the Sunday liturgy.

Gathering   The parish Eucharist begins as usual. Sometimes the sick, along with the whole congregation, are blessed with baptismal water. In Baptism we died with Christ; the suffering that these sick persons are now experiencing is part of that dying.

Storytelling   We then read from the Scriptures and hear how Christ has conquered suffering and death by his own death and resurrection.

The homily relates the readings to the Christian meaning of suffering. Those who are ill or suffering can freely and lovingly choose to unite their sufferings with the sufferings of Christ. Following the homily we join in a litany of intercession for the sick, for the parish, and for the needs of the world.

Imposition of Hands
Those to be anointed are invited to come forward. With silent and intense prayer to the Holy Spirit, the priest lays his hands on the head of each person. This is one of the key symbolic actions of the sacrament. The gesture indicates that this particular

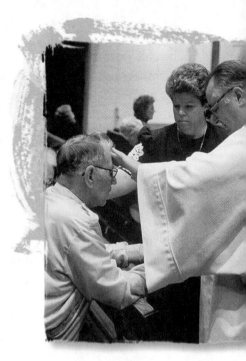

person is the object of the Church's prayer. It is a sign of blessing. Most important, it was Jesus' own gesture of healing: "At sunset, all who had people sick with various diseases brought them to him. He laid his hands on each of them and cured them" (Luke 4:40).

Invocation   The priest blesses God for the gift of oil. Olive oil reminds us of the suffering of Jesus in the Garden of Olives (Luke 22:39–46). The oil is blessed by the bishop of the diocese on Holy Thursday. It is this blessing that makes the oil sacramental.

Anointing with Oil   Next we see the essential rite of the sacrament. The priest anoints each sick person with the oil. He makes the sign of the cross first on the person's forehead and then on the palm of each hand. He prays that God in his love and mercy will "raise" the sick person to health. We all respond, "Amen."

An Exchange of Signs

The celebration of the sacrament of the Anointing of the Sick is a ritual moment that makes visible and present to the sick and to the whole community who we are as Church: a community of healing and support. That is why the whole parish community is invited to come together in prayerful support of those among us who are in special need.

The sick, in return, offer a sign to the community: In this sacrament they tell the community that they are prepared to offer their suffering, in union with Christ's, for the good of the whole Church and the salvation of the world.

This exchange of signs between the sick and the healthy members of the community is at the heart of the sacrament. The sick are assured in the ritual that their suffering is not useless, that it is a sharing in the saving work of Jesus. Their sins are forgiven. At the same time the Church asks the Lord to lighten their suffering, to give them peace and courage, and to save them.

Who can receive anointing? How sick does one have to be in order to be anointed? The Church tells us that the sacrament is for those whose health is seriously impaired by sickness or old age. One does *not* have to be in danger of death. The sacrament is most fruitful when the person being anointed is well enough to participate fully in it.

A person can be anointed before surgery when a serious illness or disability is the reason for the operation. In this case it is preferable to celebrate the sacrament even before the person goes to the hospital.

The sacrament is for all ages and all types of illness. Sick children who have sufficient use of

reason to be strengthened by the sacrament can be anointed. Persons with the disease of alcoholism or suffering from other addictions can be anointed, as can those who suffer from various mental disorders.

But the big question is, "Does it work?" Does the sick person experience healing? The answer is yes. The sacrament is the prayer of the Church, the body of Christ. Christ himself has assured us that whatever we ask the Father in his name will be granted.

In the sacrament we pray that the sick be healed in body, in soul, and in spirit. God knows more than we do what healing the sick person needs most: that a wound be healed, that a fear turn to confidence, that loneliness disappear, that bafflement in the face of all the whys—Why me? Why suffering? Why now?—may turn into understanding. Ultimately we pray that the sacrament of the Anointing of the Sick will give us a better understanding of the mystery of a loving God who raised his crucified Son, bearing his victorious wounds, to be with the Father in glory.

 Describe what you think is meant by spiritual healing.

OI stands for Oleum Infirmorum (Latin for Oil of the Sick).

Have you ever been present at the sacrament of the Anointing of the Sick? Describe the experience.

Sometimes we tend to ignore or forget about people we know who are ill. How would being prayerfully present at this sacrament help those who are not receiving it?

When is the sacrament of the Anointing of the Sick scheduled in your parish? Often at these times volunteers are needed to help care for the sick and to exercise various liturgical ministries during the celebration. Sometimes a meal is served afterward. Could you offer your help on these occasions?

In what other ways does your parish reach out to the sick? When can you take time to visit and to pray with the homebound?

YOU ARE MY WITNESSES

Scripture of My Life

As we have seen, Luke's Gospel and the Acts of the Apostles together form one work. Luke sets out to show how the mission of Jesus is continued in the work of the apostles and in the Church community through the ages. Read these parallel healing stories: Luke 5:17–26 and Acts 3:1–10. How does the Church today continue this healing ministry?

Catholic Teachings

About Viaticum

In addition to the sacrament of the Anointing of the Sick, the Church provides another great gift to those who are close to death: the Eucharist. Holy Communion given to the dying is called *Viaticum,* a word from Latin that literally means "with you on the way." Communion has a special significance when received at the close of life. "It is the seed of eternal life and the power of the resurrection" (*Catechism,* 1524).

The Sacrament of Holy Orders

How beautiful upon the mountains
are the feet of him who brings glad tidings,
Announcing peace, bearing good news.

Isaiah 52:7

The priesthood is essential to the life of the Church. Why do you think this is so?

The Call to Holy Orders

Did you know that each of us was called at Baptism to share in the priesthood of Christ? We share in his priesthood by living out our baptismal promises and by continuing Christ's work on earth. The sacraments of Baptism and Confirmation consecrate each Christian for the common priesthood of the faithful. We are not ordained ministers, but we are called to share the good news of Christ and to carry on his mission in the world.

Some, however, are called to share in Christ's priesthood in a unique way as his ordained ministers. In the sacrament of Holy Orders, men are consecrated for a special life of sacramental ministry to the body of Christ, the Church. What makes the ordained ministry different?

Holy Orders is the sacrament through which the mission and authority Christ gave his apostles continues in the Church. "The Church confers the sacrament of Holy Orders only on baptized men" (*Catechism*, 1598). The sacrament includes three ranks, or orders:

- the episcopate (bishops)
- the presbyterate (priests)
- the diaconate (deacons).

In this chapter we will look at each of these orders and examine the ways in which each is celebrated in the liturgy of the Church. In general, however, we can say that in Holy Orders a man shares in the priesthood in three essential ways: ministry, divine worship, and authority.

Ministry   Before Christ ascended into heaven, he gave his apostles this mandate:

> Go, therefore, and make disciples of all nations, baptizing them in the name of the Father, and of the Son, and of the holy Spirit, teaching them to observe all that I have commanded you. And behold, I am with you always, until the end of the age.
>
> Matthew 28:19–20

Those ordained to ministry today have the same mandate: to bring the gospel to all people and to baptize them in the name of the Trinity.

All ministry is service, and Jesus made it quite clear that his ministers were to be the servants of the Church. At the Last Supper he washed the feet of his apostles, symbolically demonstrating their call to service. He told them that he "did not come to be served but to serve" (Mark 10:45).

We read in the Acts of the Apostles that after Jesus Christ ascended to his Father and after the coming of the Holy Spirit, the apostles led the early Church in two ways:

- They traveled through the known world preaching the good news of salvation through Jesus Christ.
- They taught and passed on to the early followers of Jesus their lived memories of his words and actions, especially of his death and resurrection.

Divine Worship   The ordained ministers of the Church celebrate the Eucharist and the other sacraments with the people of God.

Priests share in Christ's priesthood to the highest degree in the Eucharist. In this divine worship they act in the person of Christ himself. They proclaim and offer to the Father Christ's paschal mystery, for "in the sacrifice of the Mass they make present again and apply, until the coming of the Lord, the unique sacrifice of the New Testament" — Christ himself (*Catechism*, 1566).

Authority   Ordained ministers share in the authority of Jesus Christ. In the gospel we see Jesus sending his disciples out to teach, to baptize, to heal, and to forgive with this authority.

After the resurrection the Church grew very rapidly as more and more people joined the Christian community. The apostles chose others to help them in their work of teaching and leading the Church in worship and service. The apostles laid their hands on them and prayed that the Holy Spirit would strengthen them. In time these successors of the apostles, as we will see, were called bishops. Bishops in turn ordained priests to help them in the work of ministry. The authority of bishops and priests comes, not from themselves, but from Jesus Christ.

Holy Orders confers an indelible mark. As in the sacraments of Baptism and Confirmation, this unique sharing in the priesthood of Christ is given only once; it cannot be repeated. One who is ordained is ordained forever.

The Apostolic Call

Jesus knew that he could not do his work for the kingdom alone. He needed helpers to carry out his mission of preaching God's love, healing the sick, and reconciling sinners. In the Gospel of Luke, we read that before choosing his apostles, Jesus "departed to the mountain to pray, and he spent the night in prayer to God. When day came, he called his disciples to himself, and from them he chose Twelve, whom he also named apostles" (Luke 6:12–13).

After the resurrection these apostles, as we know from the accounts given in the Acts of the Apostles, did carry out the work of Jesus. They were the first missionaries. They founded and guided local churches. When the need arose, they met together to consider the best decision to make for the life and growth of the Church.

In time the apostles ordained others to follow in their footsteps. From one generation to the next, new apostolic leaders have been called and ordained to service in the Church. Our bishops today are successors to the apostles, for they share to the fullest extent in the grace of Holy Orders. Bishops teach, govern, and sanctify with the authority of Christ. In his local church the bishop is the chief teacher, the chief governor, and the chief priest.

The bishop is also responsible, under the leadership of the bishop of Rome, the pope, and together with all the other bishops, for the teaching, governance, and sanctification of the entire Church throughout the world. Bishops often meet together to discuss current issues facing the Church and the world.

The Ordination of a Bishop

A bishop is ordained by other bishops. The ordination takes place during the Eucharist, after the reading of the gospel. First a mandate, or letter, from the Holy Father is read, confirming the ordination of the new bishop. Then the people of the local church are asked to give their consent to the ordination. The congregation usually responds with enthusiastic applause. A homily is given by the principal ordaining bishop. He then asks the newly chosen bishop, or bishop-elect, a series of questions. By his answers the bishop-elect declares his readiness to serve his people.

The principal ordaining bishop prays that the Lord will anoint the bishop-elect, "with the fullness of priestly grace." Then, in complete silence, he lays his hands on the head of the bishop-elect. The other bishops then do the same. This ritual action, along with the prayer of consecration, is the visible sign of the ordination of a bishop.

While the Book of the Gospels is held above the new bishop's head, the principal ordaining bishop offers the prayer of consecration. The new bishop's head is anointed with oil, the same oil used in the sacraments of Baptism and Confirmation. The Book of the Gospels, which symbolizes the bishop's role as teacher and preacher of the word of God, is then given to the new bishop.

He is also given a ring as a symbol of fidelity to the Church. He receives the miter and the crosier, or pastoral staff.

The new bishop is then invited to take his seat in the chair of the bishop, the *cathedra*, and all the bishops exchange the sign of peace.

The miter is a traditional headcovering worn by the bishop during liturgical ceremonies. The word *miter* comes from a Latin word meaning "headband." As a symbol of his office, the miter has come to signify the role of the bishop as a "herald of truth," the principal teacher of the gospel in his diocese. During the liturgy the miter is removed whenever the bishop speaks to God in prayer.

At the end of the Eucharist, the new bishop blesses the people.

Who is the bishop of your diocese? What are some ways you can support your bishop?

The Priesthood of Christ

There are many bishops and many priests, but there is only one priesthood, the priesthood of Christ. Saint Paul explained that Jesus Christ is the one priest, the one mediator between God and the human race:

> For there is one God.
> There is also one mediator between God
>   and the human race,
> Christ Jesus, himself human,
> who gave himself as ransom for all.
> 1 Timothy 2:5–6

The unique sacrifice of Jesus Christ on the cross is made present in the Eucharist. In the same way the one priesthood of Christ is made present in the priesthood of his ministers: our bishops, priests (presbyters), and deacons. This priesthood is the means that Christ chose to build up and lead the Church. Through the ordained ministry of bishops and priests, the presence of Christ as head of the Church is made visible. Through the sacrament of Holy Orders, bishops and priests are ordained to bring this unique presence of Christ to us.

Priests and bishops act not only in the name of Christ but also in the name of the whole Church, especially at the Eucharist, in which they present the entire body of Christ to God. It is because they represent Christ that they also represent the body of Christ, the Church. To share in the priesthood of Christ means to share in the work of Christ as mediator between God and the human race. It is the work of the priest, in all that he does, to serve the people of God.

In Holy Orders priests are united with the bishop in the priesthood of Christ. The priest is consecrated and ordained to preach the gospel, to celebrate the sacraments, and to guide the members of the body of Christ. He does this under the authority of his bishop.

At ordination, the new priest makes a promise of obedience to the bishop of the local church in which he will serve. At the end of the ordination rite, the bishop and the new priest exchange the sign of peace. Both actions are signs that the priest and his bishop are united in working for the kingdom of God. The bishop needs priests to help him and considers the priests of his diocese his "co-workers, his sons, his brothers and his friends" (*Catechism*, 1567).

 What do you think is the main work of a priest? Why is it essential to the Church?

The Ordination of a Priest

The ordination of a priest is very much like the ordination of a bishop. The essential rite of the sacrament—the laying on of hands and the prayer of consecration—is the same except that after the bishop lays hands on the candidate, the other priests present also lay their hands on him. This is a sign of their unity, of working together for the kingdom.

The rite of the ordination of a priest takes place during the Eucharist, after the reading of the gospel. The candidate is called forward and presented to the bishop. The bishop says:

> We rely on the help of the Lord God and our Savior Jesus Christ, and we choose this man, our brother, for priesthood in the presbyteral order.

The consent of the people is then given, usually by joyful applause. The bishop then asks the candidate, in a series of questions, if he is willing to carry out the duties of a priest. The candidate answers, "I am, with the help of God."

The candidate promises obedience to the bishop of the local church. After the bishop leads a prayer for the candidate, the candidate prostrates himself during the Litany of the Saints. The bishop asks God the Father to pour out upon the candidate the blessing of the Holy Spirit and the grace and power of the priesthood.

Then, in silence, the bishop lays his hands on the candidate's head. Still in silence, all the priests who are present also lay their hands upon the candidate. The bishop, extending his hands over the candidate, offers the prayer of consecration. These two actions—the laying on of hands followed by the prayer of consecration—are the essential signs of ordination.

The new priest is invested with the stole and chasuble as symbols of the priesthood. Next the bishop anoints the palms of the new priest's hands with chrism, the same oil used in Baptism and Confirmation. After the gifts of bread and wine are presented, the bishop gives the paten and chalice to the new priest as symbols of the mystery of the Eucharist he will celebrate.

Then the bishop and the newly ordained exchange a sign of peace, and the celebration of the Eucharist continues.

Ordained for Service

The word *deacon* comes from a Greek word meaning "to serve." The first deacons served by providing food for the poor of the early Church. We read in the Acts of the Apostles that the Church in Jerusalem was growing so quickly that the daily distribution of food was not being taken care of properly. So the apostles met with the community and said, "'It is not right for us to neglect the word of God to serve at table. Brothers, select from among you seven reputable men, filled with the Spirit and wisdom, whom we shall appoint to this task. . . .' The proposal was acceptable to the whole community" (Acts 6:2–5).

Like the deacons of the early Church, deacons today carry God's message to us and share in the mission of Christ through the grace of Holy Orders. They are marked with an indelible spiritual character that conforms them to Christ, "who made himself the 'deacon' or servant of all" (*Catechism*, 1570). Deacons today may perform their service to the Church in many ways: in assisting the bishops and priests in the

liturgy, above all in the Eucharist; in the distribution of communion; in assisting at and blessing marriages; in the proclaiming of the gospel and in preaching; in presiding over funerals; and in works of service and charity. In all these tasks the deacon is guided first of all by the bishop of the local church and then by the pastor of the parish in which he serves.

The Ordination of a Deacon

The ordination of a deacon is similar to that of a bishop or priest except that at a deacon's ordination only the bishop lays hands on the candidate. This symbolizes the deacon's special attachment to the bishop in the tasks of his service.

The ordination of a deacon, like that of a bishop and a priest, takes place at the celebration of the Eucharist. After the reading of the gospel, the candidate is called forward, the bishop is assured of his worthiness, and the people assent to ordination by enthusiastic applause. In his homily the bishop explains the role of a deacon: "He will draw new strength from the gift of the Holy Spirit. He will help the bishop and his body of priests as a minister of the word, of the altar, and of charity. He will make himself a servant to all."

The bishop lays his hands, in silence, on the candidate's head. Then, with his hands extended over the candidate, the bishop prays the prayer of consecration.

The deacon is given a deacon's stole and the special deacon's vestment called the dalmatic. He wears the stole, not around his neck as a priest does, but diagonally across his chest. Now vested as a deacon, the newly ordained minister kneels before the bishop and receives from him the Book of the Gospels, a sign that he is to teach and practice God's word.

In what ways is a deacon to be a servant and a herald?

Here is a brief summary of Holy Orders to help you recall the main ideas of this chapter.

Three Ranks	Who Ordains?	Essential Signs	Ministry
bishop (episcopate)	Only a bishop can ordain another bishop, a priest, or a deacon.	the laying on of hands and the prayer of consecration	successor to the apostles leader of his local church chief teacher, governor, and priest for his diocese in union with the pope and the other bishops, responsible for the teaching, governance, and sanctification of the entire Church
priest (presbyterate)	A priest is ordained by a bishop, usually the bishop of his diocese.	same as above	coworker with the bishop in preaching the gospel, celebrating the sacraments, and guiding the members of the body of Christ
deacon (diaconate)	A deacon is ordained by the bishop of his diocese.	same as above	assists the bishops and priests in works of service and charity and, in the liturgy, proclaiming the gospel and preaching

What do you think Jesus meant when he said that he came "not to be served but to serve"? How do ordained ministers try to serve as Christ served?

Why would you think a bishop, priest, or deacon must be a person of prayer?

Many parishes have a yearly thank-you celebration for all the people who volunteer to help the parish in every area of service. If your parish sponsors such an event, volunteer to help.

Maybe your group would like to sponsor "thank-you day" for your parish priests and deacons. You might ask one of the parish groups to help you organize it as an appreciation for those ordained to serve us in Christ day after day.

YOU ARE MY WITNESSES

Scripture & My Life

In Luke's Gospel we read that Jesus sent out the Twelve to minister to the people. Take the time to read Luke 9:1–6 to discover what the apostles were commissioned to do and what power and authority they were given.

Catholic Teachings

About the Diaconate

The order of deacon can be temporary if the man ordained deacon intends to become a priest. A *permanent deacon* is a deacon for life. A permanent deacon can be married, provided he was already married before his ordination. However, if his wife dies, he may not remarry without proper permission.

The Sacrament
of Matrimony

God is love,
and whoever remains
in love remains in God.

1 John 4:16

"A wedding lasts an hour; a marriage lasts a lifetime." What do you think this means?

The Sacrament of Matrimony

Weddings are beautiful ceremonies. Whether large or small, weddings are intended to be celebrations of love. But is there more to marriage than the feeling of romance we see so often in movies, on television, and in the books and magazines we read? Let's take a look at the wonder and mystery of marriage.

Obviously the civil authorities think there is more to marriage than movies or television portray. In the United States, for example, thousands of men and women each year obtain a civil license from the state in which they want to be married, and

each state has special requirements that must be fulfilled if a marriage is to be considered legal. These may include an age requirement or even the taking of a blood test as a check to keep society free from communicable diseases. Then every couple must go for a marriage license.

Why is the state so interested in marriage? Because marriage is so important for society. In fact society is built on marriage and the family. We as a society must know when two people are promising to share responsibility for rearing children, owning property, and paying taxes. Without marriage and family life, society would fall apart in ruins. The state wants to make sure that all is well for those who want to be married. Healthy marriages mean a healthy society everywhere in the world.

For Catholics, however, marriage goes far beyond what society demands. The Church teaches us that marriage between two baptized persons is more than a legal arrangement, more than a contract, and more than romance. Marriage is a sacrament in which a baptized man and a baptized woman commit themselves to each other as partners for life. This partnership is a sacred covenant that mirrors the relationship that Christ has with the Church.

In the *sacrament of Matrimony,* a man and woman commit themselves totally to each other in Christ. They vow to love and help each other for the rest of their lives and to share this love with their children.

In this Christian ideal of marriage, then, a man and a woman are equal partners, devoted to each other in true love, committed to each other's good, and ready to find God at the very center of their love for each other. Such a love cannot help but be open to new life—to the procreation and education of children.

This is a sacrament filled with great joy and love but it is also a serious and solemn obligation. Not everyone is ready to make such a commitment. It takes time, hard work, and deep dedication before two people are ready to walk down the aisle of a church and speak the vows of marriage to each other.

A Life-giving Sign of Grace

The sacrament of Matrimony is a life-giving sign of grace, not just at the wedding ceremony when the wedding vows are made, but for the lifetime during which the vows are lived out by a man and a woman.

Like each of the sacraments, the sacrament of Matrimony is a public act. The bride and groom speak their vows aloud before God and the community. The priest or deacon accepts these vows as the Church's official witness. There must also be two other witnesses. For a Catholic marriage to be considered valid, Catholics must marry in the presence of a priest or deacon and two witnesses. Unless otherwise dispensed, or excused, from this by the local bishop, any other marriage by Catholics would be considered invalid.

It is a surprise to many Catholics that the bride and groom themselves are the ministers of the sacrament. When the marriage vows are pronounced, the couple begins a whole new way of life. They are no longer two; they are one. The grace of this sacrament will enable them to put aside selfishness and to be open to each other in mutual support and generosity. The sacrament will strengthen them to approach an unknown future, with its joys and sorrows. It will help them to build their family life on the rock foundation of faith in Christ.

 The banns of marriage are customary in the Church. The word *banns* means "proclamations" or "announcements." For three weeks before a wedding, the parish prints in the weekly bulletin or announces at Mass the names of the bride and groom and the date of the wedding. Because we are a community, we need to know when our sisters and brothers in faith are taking this decisive step in their lives. When you read or hear the banns of marriage, pray for those entering into this beautiful sacramental commitment.

they are still immature. Others fail to work at marriage. Those who succeed at marriage are those who work at the kind of love Saint Paul describes, a love that "bears all things, believes all things, hopes all things, endures all things" (1 Corinthians 13:7).

Think about important events in your life that have taken preparation on your part. Why is preparation for marriage so important?

Getting Ready

When a couple decides to marry, it is because they have chosen to spend the rest of their lives together. They become engaged and announce their intention to marry. When one or both of them is Catholic, they meet with the parish priest, deacon, or other minister to begin a time of preparation. The sacrament of Matrimony requires special preparation because of the serious nature of the commitment. The couple must know of marriage's responsibilities, challenges, and graces. No one must enter into marriage lightly or without thought.

The priest or deacon will help the couple to determine whether or not they truly are free to marry to be certain that nothing or no one holds them back from making a free commitment in love. When we marry, we promise fidelity to one person with a permanent commitment. Marriage is not something that we try out for a while! We promise to be true to the other "in good times and in bad, in sickness and in health" until death.

Sadly, some people cannot make this type of commitment in Christ. Others try too early when

Real Love

Catholics can never take the attitude that "we can always divorce if it doesn't go well." We believe that the sacrament of Matrimony forms an *indissoluble bond*—a bond that can never be broken. Real love based in Christ is not here one day and gone the next; real love is forever.

Celebrating Matrimony

Like every other sacrament Matrimony reveals something of the paschal mystery. When two Catholics celebrate the sacrament of Matrimony, they celebrate their willingness to imitate and encounter Christ in their lives of service, in the dyings and risings, sorrows and joys of family life.

The meaning of Catholic marriage is expressed in the rite of marriage. It is most fitting that the rite be

indissolubility, that is, lifelong faithfulness; and in *openness to having children*. These three qualities are essential to Christian marriage.

Meal Sharing   As we have seen, when two practicing Catholics exchange their vows, they usually do so in the context of the Eucharist at a nuptial Mass. All that marriage says about union with Christ in sacrificial love is said even more eloquently in the Eucharist.

Commissioning   The blessing at the end of Mass is directed especially to the bride and groom. One blessing asks that the peace of Christ may always be in their home.

Recall a wedding liturgy in which you have participated. Can you describe the main elements based on the outline given here?

celebrated with a nuptial Mass. In this way the bride and groom unite themselves to the self-offering of Christ in the Eucharist. It is also fitting that they receive the Body and Blood of Christ in Holy Communion, which seals their union in Christ.

The sacrament of Matrimony has the same basic shape as all the other sacraments.

Gathering   The priest or deacon greets the bride and groom, welcoming them and their families and friends in the name of the Church.

Storytelling   The couple often selects the Scripture passages from the rite that correspond to the religious meaning they wish to express in their wedding.

Exchange of Vows   It is the bride and groom who, by their free consent and mutual vows, are the ministers of the sacrament. The pledging of vows must be *witnessed* by a priest, the Church's official witness, and two other people, usually the maid of honor and the best man. The free consent of the couple and the presence of a priest and two witnesses are the essential signs of the sacrament. The bride and groom stand before the congregation and vow "to give themselves, each to the other, mutually and definitively, in order to live a covenant of faithful and fruitful love" (*Catechism*, 1662).

The couple must reflect God's faithful love in three ways: in *unity* of body, heart, and soul; in

Are You Ready for Marriage?

The correct answer to the question above is, of course, no. Readiness for a lifelong commitment demands a certain maturity, an ability to care for and support a family, and an awareness of the challenges and responsibilities that joining one's life to another's demands. Still most of you are, whether you know it or not, preparing for marriage right now.

As we grow through life, we become aware of our own unique characteristics. Some of these we can do nothing about. The color of our hair and eyes is based on genetics, not personal preference. Other characteristics, however, are not fixed forever. We can make decisions about our personality traits. We can decide, for example, to be kind, to be more patient, to listen to others, to keep our promises. In other words, we can begin now to decide what kind of person we want to become, what kind of interpersonal skills we want to learn.

The vocation of marriage requires interpersonal skills. Marriage is a union of two compatible but often very different people. Two unique personalities must learn to make important decisions together, to discuss their differences of opinion, to allow themselves to reveal deep feelings to the other. This is not easy for anyone!

107

The following questionnaire is a sample of the kinds of questions engaged couples are asked. Such a questionnaire can help the couple to become more aware of their own personalities and their ability to communicate with others. You have probably used these skills in friendships, in groups or teams you might belong to, or in group projects in school. Everyone needs these skills. Those who work on developing their interpersonal skills are headed toward satisfying friendships and, in time, a good marriage.

You may want to write your personal responses to these questions in your journal and then share your ideas and solutions in small groups. Check those skills you wish to improve.

MY INTERPERSONAL SKILLS

☐ Am I a good listener? How do I show this?

☐ How do I deal with criticism?

☐ What do I do when I am angry? How do I solve the problem?

☐ Do I spend money wisely?

☐ Do I give positive feedback? Do I affirm others and thank them when I am grateful for their help or support?

☐ Do I talk over problems with the person or persons directly involved?

☐ If I have a serious problem or need, do I talk it over with an adult I can trust?

☐ Do I look for ways to help others when I can?

☐ Do I show respect for others in my speech, saying "please," "thank you," and "pardon me"?

☐ Do I apologize when I've made a mistake or caused a problem?

☐ What is my reaction when my plans are upset for some reason?

☐ Have I learned to play with and watch over young children safely?

☐ Do I speak with adults respectfully and courteously?

☐ How do I treat the elderly persons I meet?

 How do you think developing interpersonal skills can prepare you for marriage?

What do you think makes a good marriage?

What makes a marriage Catholic? Why are the bride and groom the ministers of the sacrament?

Why does the Church urge that Catholics be married at a nuptial Mass?

Each parish provides some form of preparation for those who wish to marry. Some parishes put the prospective bride and groom in contact with a Catholic couple who have been living the sacrament for a number of years. Some parishes provide Pre-Cana courses or Engaged Encounter weekends. What form of preparation for marriage is provided by your parish? What does it involve?

YOU ARE MY WITNESSES

Scripture of My Life

The Church provides a variety of Scripture readings for the rite of marriage. Find the passages listed here. Then choose one. What does it tell you about the sacrament of Matrimony?

1 Corinthians 12:31—13:8
1 John 4:7–12
Ephesians 5:2, 25–32

Catholic Teachings

About "Openness to Children"

The Church teaches that the gift of sex is given to human beings so that two people can become one in love and intimacy and companionship and that the natural outcome of responsible and faithful love is new life—children. That is why anything which blocks this purpose artificially, such as condoms or birth control devices, is forbidden. The Church does not forbid natural methods of birth control, however.

Mary and the Saints

Lord, this is the people that
longs to see your face.

Solemnity of All Saints

All Christian prayer is directed
to God the Father in the name of Jesus.
Our Catholic tradition is filled with prayers calling upon
the saints and uniquely upon Mary the mother of Jesus.
Why do Catholics call upon Mary and the
saints to intercede for us?

The Communion of Saints

Sometimes on headstones in a cemetery, there is a request: "Please pray for me," or "Pray for the repose of the soul of. . . ." We find such inscriptions in the early Christian cemeteries, too.

On the tombs of the martyrs, however, the inscriptions are different: They ask the martyrs to pray for us! These inscriptions are our earliest evidence of Christian prayer to the saints. From the beginning Christians have called upon Mary and the saints to intercede with God for them. Why?

In the preface for Masses on saints' days, we thank God because:

You renew the Church in every age
by raising up men and women outstanding in
  holiness,
living witnesses of your unchanging love.
They inspire us by their heroic lives,
and help us by their constant prayers
to be the living sign of your saving power.

We honor the saints because of their example and their intercession. They show us how to follow Christ, and they help us by their prayers.

The holiness of the saints is a reflection of God's holiness. In the sacraments the Father shares his holiness with us through the Son and the Holy

112

Spirit. Through the sacraments we enter into a "holy communion" and share, in union with the saints, God's life. Our union with God's holiness and with his holy ones (the saints) is called the *communion of saints*.

The doctrine of the communion of saints has very important consequences for our daily lives. Think of what it means — we are united with the saints in a common holiness!

Think, for a moment, of your physical body. When you exercise and strengthen your arms, your whole body benefits. When you do aerobics to strengthen your lungs and your heart, your whole body benefits. So it is with the body of Christ. "Since all the faithful form one body, the good of each is communicated to the others" (*Catechism*, 947).

Because we are members of the same body of Christ, all the good works, the merits, and the graces of the saints are communicated to us. The communion of saints assures us that *together* we form one family in Christ. What an encouragement this can be as we struggle and often fail in our efforts to follow Jesus. God's holiness is a *shared* gift.

What, then, does holiness mean for each one of us? We grow in holiness through a continual process of turning our lives toward God. We keep trying to empty ourselves of selfishness and sin in order to allow God's Spirit to fill us and to work in us. The saints have accomplished this to such a degree that when we look at their lives, we see and understand what Saint Paul meant when he wrote, "I live, no longer I, but Christ lives in me" (Galatians 2:20).

The communion of saints is both a tremendous responsibility and a source of great hope. Our responsibility is to follow Christ faithfully, as members of his body. Our hope is that we, together with all the saints, will share eternally in his final victory.

 How can you build up the communion of saints?

Celebrating the Saints

Devotion to Our Lady and the saints goes back to the earliest days of our Church. There is a rich liturgical tradition in the Church that celebrates Mary and the lives of the saints.

Liturgical celebrations are divided into three degrees. The most important days are called *solemnities*. For example, the days on which we celebrate the Trinity, Our Lord, or the Holy Spirit—Trinity Sunday, Christmas, Easter, Pentecost — are solemnities. In addition, we celebrate eight solemnities in honor of Mary or the saints each year. These include the solemnities of Mary, the Mother of God (January 1); Joseph, patron of the universal Church (March 19); John the Baptist (June 24); and the Apostles Peter and Paul (June 29).

Second in order of importance is that of *feast*. This rank includes, among others, the feasts of apostles and evangelists; the feast of the angels and archangels (September 29); and the feast of the first martyr, Stephen (December 26).

The final rank is *memorial*. On memorial days we celebrate the *memory* of a saint. Just as you might mark the birthdays of your friends on your calendar, the Church marks the birthdays of individual saints. However, there is one important difference. The Church does not celebrate the day the saints were born on earth but instead the day on which they were born into eternal life—that is, the day on which they died. It is their passage into new and eternal life that we celebrate, affirming that Christ's victory over death became fully real in their lives.

Reflections of the Holy

What does it mean when we call someone a *saint*? The word means "holy." In order to understand the holiness of the saints, we must start with the realization that only God is holy. If we call anyone other than God "holy," it is because the person reflects God's holiness. When we honor a saint's achievements, we are honoring what God did through the saint. Holiness is achieved, not by doing great things, but by allowing God's greatness to work in us.

113

The Church is aware that millions of Christians have lived holy lives and that they now share in the happiness of God's life in heaven. They are all saints in the general sense of the word. However, in order to recognize the holiness of particular saints in a formal way, the Church has instituted the process called *canonization.* In order for a holy person to be canonized, a careful investigation is made of the person's life. The final results are sent to the Congregation for the Causes of Saints in Rome. The holy person may then be given the title of "Blessed."

Usually, three miracles attributed to the holy person's intercession are required before formal declaration of sainthood. Then the pope, in a beautiful and solemn ceremony, canonizes the saint, declaring that this holy person is truly a saint and extending veneration of this newly canonized saint to the whole Church.

The diversity in the lives of the saints teaches us that all Christians are called to holiness by imitating Christ in their particular circumstances. The life stories of the saints can often help us face the challenges in our own lives. And these great heroes and heroines can become our role models in living the Christian life.

Mary, Mother of Jesus

Mary has been honored in many ways through the centuries. However, everything that can be said about Mary, all the honor given to her, is due to two important facts: She is the mother of Jesus, and she is his first disciple. By understanding these two relationships, we can understand the role Mary plays in our salvation.

First of all, we honor Mary because of her relationship to Jesus: She is his mother. Mary does not draw attention to herself; she always points to Jesus. Each of the honors given to

Blessed Katharine Drexel

Mary is best understood in relation to Christ. We can see this in the four principal privileges for which the Church has traditionally honored Mary: Mother of God, the Blessed Virgin, the Immaculate Conception, and the Assumption.

What we believe about Mary is based on our understanding of Jesus. For example, when the second Council of Ephesus (A.D. 431) proclaimed Mary the Mother of God, it was declaring who *Jesus* was. The child that Mary bore in her womb was divine and therefore Mary, the mother of that child, is indeed the Mother of God. We celebrate the Solemnity of Mary, Mother of God on January 1.

We call Mary the Blessed Virgin because the Church has always believed and taught that Jesus was conceived by the power of the Holy Spirit.

Because God chose Mary to be the Mother of the Savior, it is fitting that she was the first to be saved. We believe that she was redeemed and free from all sin from the very beginning of her life—that is, from the moment of her conception. We call this privilege the immaculate conception. We celebrate the Solemnity of the Immaculate Conception on December 8.

We believe that when Mary's life on earth was over, God took her into heaven body and soul.

Saint Frances Xavier Cabrini

Saint Charles Lwanga

This participation in the resurrection and ascension of her son is called the assumption of the Blessed Virgin. We celebrate the Solemnity of the Assumption on August 15.

Mary, First Disciple of Jesus

The second reason we honor Mary is because of her relation to the Church: Mary is the first member of the Church, the model disciple. What does it mean to be a disciple? A disciple follows Jesus in doing the will of his Father.

No one has lived this more perfectly than Mary. Mary shows us what it means to be a disciple of Jesus, what it means to be a member of the Church.

We, too, are disciples. Mary, as Mother of God, bore Jesus in her womb and gave him birth. Today we, the Church, bear Christ in our bodies by Baptism and Eucharist. We are to bring forth Christ to our world by word and example. This is how we live as Jesus' disciples.

 What does Mary's life say to you about discipleship?

Blessed Juan Diego

Saint Andrew Kim

The Hail Mary

The most common prayer to Mary, the one all Catholics know by heart, is the Hail Mary.

The prayer consists of two greetings and a petition. The two greetings are taken from the first chapter of Luke's Gospel. The first is the greeting of the angel Gabriel (Luke 1:28); the second, that of Mary's cousin Elizabeth (Luke 1:42).

The greeting of the angel Gabriel reminds us of the Book of Zephaniah: "Shout for joy, O daughter Zion! . . . The LORD your God is in your midst" (Zephaniah 3:14, 17). In the Hail Mary we pray, "Hail Mary, full of grace, the Lord is with you." The word we translate as "Hail" is the same word Zephaniah used: "Rejoice" or "Shout for joy." In Gabriel's greeting to Mary, it is as if he were saying to her, "Shout for joy, O highly favored one! The Lord is in your midst."

CATHOLIC ID Do you have a patron saint? The Church encourages Catholics to be given the name of a saint when they are baptized as infants. Parents are not required to name their child after a saint, but it is an excellent tradition. A patron saint serves as an example of Christian life, and the child who is given a saint's name is assured of the saint's intercession.

Catholics may also choose another saint's name when they are confirmed. They do this in order to have another personal example of the Christian life to imitate. Today, however, some Catholics keep their baptismal names when they are confirmed in order to emphasize the connection between Baptism and Confirmation.

Blessed Kateri Tekakwitha

115

Some of the many cultural representations of the Blessed Virgin Mary in art

When we say "Hail Mary," then, it is helpful to remember that this greeting is a joyful reminder of God's goodness and favor: Shout for joy!

The second greeting of the Hail Mary is that of Elizabeth: "Most blessed are you among women, and blessed is the fruit of your womb" (Luke 1:42). Mary is always seen in relation to her son. As Jesus is the source of every blessing, Mary, who bore Jesus in her womb and brought him forth to the world, is indeed worthy to be called blessed.

The second half of the Hail Mary is a traditional prayer of petition whose origins are lost in history. In it we ask that Mary will intercede for us "now and at the hour of our death."

The Rosary

There came a time when many Christians no longer knew the psalms by heart, so they began to meditate on the life of Jesus while reciting the Hail Mary or the Lord's Prayer. Eventually this practice was called praying the rosary. By the fifteenth century it had become a popular devotion.

The rosary can be prayed alone or with others. Usually we start with the Apostles' Creed, one Our Father, three Hail Marys, and one Glory to the Father. Following this introduction, we begin our meditation on the mysteries. Meditation—thinking and praying about the wonderful events of our salvation—is at the very heart of the rosary.

Each decade of the rosary is made up of one Our Father, ten Hail Marys, and one Glory to the Father. At the beginning of each decade, we select the mystery on which we are going to meditate. Then we think of this event in the life of Jesus or in the life of his mother while praying the ten Hail Marys. We usually end the Rosary with a centuries-old prayer to Mary, the Hail, Holy Queen.

Recall the words of Gabriel and Elizabeth to Mary: joy and blessing. Then quietly pray the Hail Mary together.

Things to SHARE

What difference should the communion of saints make in our lives as Catholics?

What is your favorite Scripture story about Mary?

Each parish church has a "title;" that is, it is named after the Trinity or Our Lord (or a mystery in his life), the Holy Spirit, the Blessed Virgin Mary, one of the angels, or a saint. What is the title of your parish church? Is it named after a saint? When is this title celebrated? What special things are done on that day?

Some parishes offer a calendar to parishioners each year. On this calendar are marked all the saints' days and seasons of the year. Look up your birthday. What saint shares this day with you?

YOU ARE MY WITNESSES

Scripture of My Life

Most of the mysteries of the rosary come from the gospel accounts in the Scripture. The *joyful mysteries* are the annunciation, visitation, nativity, presentation, and finding in the Temple. The *sorrowful mysteries* are the agony in the garden, scourging, crowning with thorns, carrying of the cross, and crucifixion. The *glorious mysteries* are the resurrection, ascension, descent of the Holy Spirit, assumption of Mary, and coronation of Mary.

Pray a decade of the rosary this week. Choose a mystery for meditation and end the decade by praying the Hail, Holy Queen (page 125).

CATHOLIC TEACHINGS

About Adoration

We use the words *adoration* and *worship* only when speaking of God, Jesus Christ, and the Holy Spirit. We do not use these words in reference to Mary, the other saints, or any blessed image or object. As Catholics we honor the saints; we venerate them; we recall their memory and express our devotion to them. But we do not worship statues or adore the saints. Adoration is for God alone.

Paths of Prayer

You will show me the path to life,
abounding joy in your presence.

Psalm 16:11

Prayer is a path that leads
to God; prayer is a window that reflects
God's light; prayer is a heart open to God's love.
What is prayer for you?

Windows of Prayer

In *prayer* we raise our hearts and minds to God. We ask God for the good things we need, we thank him for his gifts, we express our sorrow for sin, we pray for others, and we praise him for his goodness. With the help of the Holy Spirit and the tradition of the Church, we can pray in many ways. Here is one you might like to try.

Look at the empty stained-glass window here. How would you complete it? Here is a suggestion: Make this window into an expression of your relationship with God. Like a stained-glass window, this relationship has many dimensions. Think about the sacraments you have celebrated; you may want to symbolize each one in a section of your window. Think about your times of prayer, both during the liturgy and alone. These could be symbolized in sections of your window. How do family and friends help you find God? Symbolize this in your window. Perhaps the Scriptures will find a place in your window as well.

What would you put in the center of your window? Perhaps you might insert a symbol of Jesus: the cross as symbol of the paschal mystery or bread and wine, the symbols of the Eucharist. What symbolizes the center of your relationship with God?

Praying with Scripture

The Sacred Scriptures can enrich our prayer immensely. They are the "faith record" of God's mysterious plan—what God has done in history and the revelation of God's plan for the world. A good way to pray is to take the Bible, read a passage, and then talk it over with God.

Praying with just one or two Scripture verses is a traditional and practical way to make prayer a part of our everyday lives. We can easily pray a short, easy-to-remember Scripture verse at work or play or during those "between times" we find ourselves in so often: between home and school, between lunch and recess, between the ending of one class and the beginning of another.

Here are several ways to pray with Scripture. Which appeal to you?

The Our Father

The whole gospel of Jesus Christ is summed up in the Our Father. It is the purest and most essential prayer of the Church. When we pray the Our Father, we pray with the attitude of Jesus and the Spirit of Jesus. We pray for what Jesus wants— that God's will be done on earth. As we pray the Our Father, we become one with Jesus and one with the Father in love and trust. The Our Father can be found in Matthew 6:9–13 and in Luke 11:2–4.

Scripture Pictures

When people asked Saint Ignatius Loyola for help in prayer, he advised them to picture a scene from Scripture and to put themselves into the scene. Try it with Matthew 8:23–27. Imagine the people, the sounds, the smells; and especially, see Jesus as he speaks and acts. What is he saying to you? When you finish, write your thoughts in your journal.

God's Word for the Day

Compile a list of at least seven favorite Scripture passages. Choose one each day as your special verse. Every time your mind is free or you are between activities, recall your verse and say it to yourself a few times. Here are two for your list:

- "Your word is a lamp for my feet,
  a light for my path" (Psalm 119:105).
- "I am the good shepherd, and I know mine and mine know me" (John 10:14).

Today's Scripture

Using the Church's calendar of Scripture readings, find the readings for today. Read them and the psalm carefully. If you find a verse or idea meaningful, stop and let it sink in. Stay with it as long as you like. Then go on. Choose one of the verses, and recall it often during the day.

Scripture and Music

Music is a traditional and beautiful way to focus on the words and meaning of Scripture. Try setting a favorite verse to a simple melody, perhaps in a chantlike style. Create a harmony as well! You may want to use a Scripture story or set of verses as the basis for an entire song. Saint John Chrysostom wrote many Scripture hymns for the Church. Ask his help!

Scripture Exchange

Spend some time looking through the New Testament. Write down, on an index card or a slip of paper, one or two verses you like. Collect them from the group in a box or basket. Then invite each group member to draw one. You may want to decorate or illustrate your verse on paper and display it.

The Prayer of the Name

"You shall name him Jesus" (Luke 1:31). The name of Jesus is a simple but powerful prayer, and using the holy name of Jesus in prayer is an ancient tradition in the Church. Begin by closing your eyes and becoming still. Breathe slowly and deeply. Then, as you breathe in, quietly say "Jesus." As you breathe out, you may want to say "Savior" or "peace" or another word that reminds you of Jesus. Continue this rhythm for as long as you wish.

Scriptural Meditation

The path of meditation is another path to union with God. *Meditation* is simply "thinking about God," and it can easily flow into *contemplation* ("being with" God). Most often we meditate on the Scriptures, but other spiritual books can be starting points as well, especially those that explain the Scriptures and inspire us to live the Christian life. A scriptural meditation has been prepared for you on the next page.

A Scripture Meditation

For now, let's choose a Scripture passage, Mark 10:46–52, for our meditation. Before meditating, it is a good idea to help yourself become calm, peaceful, and undistracted. Sometimes listening to soft background music can help. First sit in a straight but comfortable position and close your eyes. Now let's try it.

Imagine yourself sitting by the side of a dusty road. You look down the road. You are waiting for Jesus to come by. Already you see him in the distance, surrounded by a large crowd.

Suddenly, across the road, you notice someone—Bartimaeus, a blind man. He, too, is waiting for Jesus. You hear him call out, "Jesus, Son of David, have pity on me." Jesus and the crowd are coming closer. What do you hear? There is the calling of Bartimaeus, the buzz of the crowd, and someone scolding Bartimaeus: "Quiet, blind man!" What do you see? There is Jesus, coming down the road. There is Bartimaeus, alone and poor, the hot sun beating down on him.

Suddenly all is silent. Jesus is here—just a few feet away. "Call him," Jesus says. Someone runs to where Bartimaeus sits in the sun. "Take courage; get up, he is calling you."

Everything is happening right in front of you. You see Bartimaeus as he joyfully throws aside his cloak, springs to his feet, and comes to Jesus. You hear Jesus ask, "What do you want me to do for you?" Bartimaeus replies in a pleading voice, "Master, I

want to see." Jesus tells him, "Go your way; your faith has saved you." Immediately Bartimaeus receives his sight and begins to follow Jesus.

But wait! Jesus is stopping again. He has seen you sitting there in your special place. Jesus calls to you, "Come here, my friend." You quickly stand up and go to meet him. Jesus looks at you with great love. "So—why were you waiting for me? What do you want me to do for you?"

Think a moment. What is your answer? What does Jesus say to you?

Take time to "just be with" Jesus a little while.

Now begin to say good-bye. Watch Jesus a moment as he turns to continue his journey of healing. Now begin your own journey back. Say good-bye to your special place. Then open your eyes slowly. Let us pray the Our Father together.

A Life of Prayer

In our Catholic life of prayer, we often pray with words, aloud, and usually with others. This prayer with words is called *vocal prayer* because we pray

LOOKING BACK

Think for a moment about your experience. If there is anything about your meditation that you would like to remember, write it in your journal now.

In prayer God always gives us exactly what we need. All prayer is a gift of God's life and grace. We need only take time to receive it.

not only with our minds and hearts but with our voices as well. The prayers we say during the liturgy are vocal prayers, as are traditional prayers such as the Our Father and the Hail Mary.

There are many paths to God in prayer. Vocal prayer is one of them. Once two sisters asked Saint Teresa of Avila how to find union with God. "Say the Our Father," responded Teresa. Sometimes when we say a familiar prayer carefully and thoughtfully, we gain insight into the meaning of the words. Then the words slowly fade away, and we find ourselves "just being" at peace in God. This is the prayer of contemplation.

Contemplation is the prayer of union with God. We might also call it the prayer of "just being with" God. If you look up the word *contemplation* in the dictionary, you will find: "the act of looking at attentively and thoughtfully." The prayer of contemplation is simply looking at God. As one saint described this kind of prayer, "I look at God and he looks at me."

We can also pray with sacramentals. Sacramentals are part of our daily lives. They are blessings, actions, and objects that the Church uses to prepare us for the graces of the sacraments. By objects, we mean things such as statues, medals, rosaries, candles, and crucifixes. By actions, we mean actions such as the sign of the cross, the laying on of hands, the sprinkling of blessed water. Blessings include the blessing of people, places, food, and objects. We bless ashes on Ash Wednesday and palms on Palm Sunday. Can you think of other times when we use blessings?

Unlike sacraments, which were instituted by Christ, sacramentals were instituted by the Church. The Church teaches us that sacramentals are never to be used in a magical or superstitious way or looked upon as good luck charms.

What sacramentals are part of your everyday life? You may want to write your own prayer, asking God's blessing on yourself, your family, your home, and your everyday activities.

PRAYERS

*With your right thumb,
trace a small cross on your lips and say:*

LORD, OPEN MY LIPS,
AND MY MOUTH WILL
proclaim your praise.

UPON WAKING

OUR FATHER,
WHO ART IN HEAVEN,
hallowed be thy name;
thy kingdom come;
thy will be done on earth as it is
in heaven.
Give us this day our daily bread;
and forgive us our trespasses
as we forgive those who trespass
against us;
and lead us not into temptation,
but deliver us from evil.
Amen.

OUR FATHER

MY GOD,
I AM SORRY FOR MY SINS WITH ALL MY HEART.
In choosing to do wrong
and failing to do good,
I have sinned against you
whom I should love above all things.
I firmly intend, with your help,
to do penance,
to sin no more,
and to avoid whatever leads me to sin.
Our Savior Jesus Christ
suffered and died for us.
In his name, my God, have mercy.

ACT OF CONTRITION

COME, HOLY SPIRIT,
FILL THE HEARTS OF YOUR FAITHFUL.
And kindle in them the fire of your love.

Send forth your Spirit and they shall be created.
And you will renew the face of the earth.

Let us pray.

Lord,
by the light of the Holy Spirit
you have taught the hearts of your faithful.
In the same Spirit
help us to relish what is right
and always rejoice in your consolation.

We ask this through Christ our Lord.
Amen.

PRAYER TO THE HOLY SPIRIT

ETERNAL REST
GRANT UNTO THEM,
O Lord.

And let perpetual light shine upon them.
May they rest in peace.
Amen.

May their souls and the souls of all the
faithful departed, through the mercy of
God, rest in peace.
Amen.

May the angels lead you into paradise;
may the martyrs come to welcome you
and take you to the holy city,
the new and eternal Jerusalem.

PRAYERS FOR THE DECEASED
FROM THE ORDER OF
CHRISTIAN FUNERALS

124

HAIL MARY, FULL OF GRACE,
THE LORD IS WITH YOU!

Blessed are you among women,
and blessed is the fruit of your womb, Jesus.
Holy Mary, Mother of God,
pray for us sinners,
now and at the hour of our death.
Amen.

HAIL MARY

HAIL, HOLY QUEEN,
MOTHER OF MERCY,

hail, our life, our sweetness, and our hope.
To you we cry, the children of Eve;
to you we send up our sighs,
mourning and weeping in this land of exile.
Turn, then, most gracious advocate,
your eyes of mercy toward us;
lead us home at last
and show us the blessed fruit of your womb,
Jesus:
O clement, O loving, O sweet Virgin Mary.

HAIL HOLY QUEEN

JESUS,
YOU ARE GOD-WITH-US,

especially in this sacrament
of the Eucharist.
You love me as I am
and help me grow.

Come and be with me
in all my joys and sorrows.
Help me share your peace and love
with everyone I meet.

PRAYER BEFORE COMMUNION

JESUS, SON OF GOD,
THANKS AND PRAISE TO YOU.

Jesus, Good Shepherd,
    thanks and praise to you.
Jesus, Lamb of God,
    thanks and praise to you.
Jesus, Bread of life and love,
    thanks and praise to you.
Jesus, Source of strength and joy,
    thanks and praise to you.

Thank you, Jesus, for your life
in mine. Help me live your good
news of love and peace.

PRAYER AFTER COMMUNION

HOLY DAYS OF OBLIGATION

SOLEMNITY OF MARY,
MOTHER OF GOD
(January 1)

ASCENSION
(during the Easter season)

ASSUMPTION OF MARY
(August 15)

ALL SAINTS' DAY
(November 1)

IMMACULATE CONCEPTION
(December 8)

CHRISTMAS
(December 25)

THE LITURGICAL YEAR

"Christ's saving work is celebrated in sacred memory by the Church on fixed days throughout the year. Each week on the day called the Lord's Day the Church commemorates the Lord's resurrection. Once a year at Easter the Church honors this resurrection and passion with the utmost solemnity. In fact through the yearly cycle the Church unfolds the entire mystery of Christ and keeps the anniversaries of the saints" (General Norms for the Liturgical Year and the Calendar, 1).

The liturgy makes every day of our lives holy, especially when we celebrate the Eucharist and pray the divine office. We celebrate Sunday first of all, because Sunday is the day of the Lord's resurrection.

THE EASTER TRIDUUM

The three days of the Easter Triduum are the most important days of the entire liturgical year; during these days we celebrate the passion and resurrection of Jesus. The Easter Triduum begins with the evening Mass of the Lord's Supper on Holy Thursday. Its high point is the Easter Vigil. The Triduum ends with evening prayer on Easter Sunday.

The Easter Vigil celebrates the "blessed night" when Christ rose from the dead. The Church keeps watch as it awaits Christ's resurrection and welcomes new members of the body of Christ. The entire celebration of this vigil must take place at night.

THE EASTER SEASON

The fifty days from Easter Sunday to Pentecost are celebrated as one "great Sunday." These are the days we sing *Alleluia* and rejoice in our salvation.

THE SEASON OF LENT

During Lent we prepare to celebrate Easter. The liturgy of Lent reminds us of our Baptism. Catechumens prepare for the sacraments of initiation. All Catholics are urged to pray, fast, give alms, and do acts of penance.

THE SEASON OF ADVENT

The liturgical year begins with the first Sunday of Advent. Advent is a time of preparation for Christmas and for Christ's second coming at the end of time. We recall the long years of waiting by the people of Israel for the Messiah, and the faithfulness of Mary and Joseph to God's plan.

THE SEASON OF CHRISTMAS

Christmas is our celebration of Jesus' birth. It begins at the Vigil Mass on Christmas Eve and ends on the feast of the Baptism of the Lord. The season includes the events from Jesus' birth to the beginning of his public ministry.

ORDINARY TIME

Ordinary Time in the Church's year occurs between the Christmas and Lenten seasons, and after the Easter Season until the beginning of Advent. Ordinary Time is devoted to the mystery of Christ in all its aspects.

In this yearly cycle, we also venerate with a special love Mary, the Mother of God. We celebrate the memory of the martyrs and other saints. On Saturdays in Ordinary Time, if there is no obligatory memorial to a saint, a memorial of the Blessed Virgin Mary may be celebrated.

The liturgical year ends with the solemnity of Christ the King, the last Sunday in Ordinary Time.

REMEMBER

126

Index